ENFORCING ANTITRUST AGAINST FOREIGN ENTERPRISES

# ENFORCING ANTITRUST AGAINST FOREIGN ENTERPRISES

## Procedural Problems in the Extraterritorial Application of Antitrust laws

Report submitted to Committee C – Antitrust Law and Monopolies during the IBA Berlin Conference, August 1980

General Rapporteur, Cornelis Canenbley, Düsseldorf, with the assistance of Amanda Dalton, London.

This General Report has been prepared on the basis of, and in cooperation with, national reports from:



| | | |
|---|---|---|
| Australia | – | Kerry M. Wright, Sydney |
| EEC | – | Mario Siragusa, Brussels |
| France | – | Dominique Voillemot, Paris |
| Germany | – | Jochen Burrichter, Düsseldorf |
| Italy | – | Giuseppe Bisconti, Rome |
| Switzerland | – | Michel Haymann, Zürich |
| U.K. | – | Neville March Hunnings, London |
| USA | – | Mark R. Joelson, Washington D.C. |
| | | Joseph P. Griffin, Washington D.C. |



1981
KLUWER - DEVENTER - THE NETHERLANDS
BOSTON . ANTWERP . LONDON . FRANKFURT

**Library of Congress Cataloging in Publication Data**

Canenbley, Cornelis, 1942-
Enforcing antitrust against foreign enterprises.

'Report submitted to Committee C – Antitrust Law and Monopolies during the IBA Berlin Conference, August 1980.'
1. Conflict of laws – Antitrust law. I. Dalton, Amanda. II. International Bar Association. Committee C – Antitrust Law and Monopolies. III. Title.

| | | |
|---|---|---|
| K7582.M6C36 | 343'.072 | 81-12327 |
| ISBN 90 654 4014 3 | 342.372 | AACR2 |

# Foreword

One of the basic problems of any legal system in history has been and still is the question how far any national law may be applied to and enforced against conduct committed outside its territory. Although of relevance in any field of law this problem has become a major issue in the field of antitrust law during this century and especially since 1945. For as many different economic systems and concepts about the role of competition in economy exist world-wide conflicts between the different systems have become unavoidable the more integration of the various economies by world trade increased.

The Committee on Antitrust Law and Monopolies of the International Bar Association's Section on Business Law therefore has during the last years on various occasions discussed the famous subject of 'extraterritorial application of antitrust laws'. A special part of this subject is the question how far one country's antitrust laws even if applicable in substance may be in fact enforced against foreign citizens. Therefore 'procedural problems with regard to the extraterritorial application of antitrust laws' was one topic of the Committee's meetings during the IBA Conference in Berlin 1980.

As chairman of the Committee I want to express my sincere thanks to Dr. Cornelis Canenbley, Düsseldorf, the general rapporteur for the excellent report which was the basis of our discussion in Berlin. May I extend my thanks to all national rapporteurs who have provided valuable contributions under their respective national laws. I am convinced that the publication of this general report and as far as possible parts of national reports too will provide a useful guide for all international lawyers who have to deal with such cases. In order to increase this usefulness a number of legal texts have been added which might be of special interest in this connection.

*Professor Arved Deringer*
Chairman Committee on Antitrust Law
and Monopolies

Cologne, February 1981

# Introduction

Many people – some lawyers amongst them – are not particularly interested in the subject of 'procedure'. They prefer to leave this somewhat dry area of law to specialists.

In practice, however, the substantive scope of national or supranational legal provisions may be less important than the attendant procedural ones. The practical problems and political implications arise when – in an individual case – authorities, courts or even private persons of one state try to enforce their law in situations in which conflicts with the interests or possibly even with the law of a foreign state exist. Perhaps the best illustration of this and one which demonstrates the practical importance of this Report is the well known Westinghouse Uranium Litigation, a factual summary of which is attached as Appendix 8, and the SNPE case on which an article by Dr. A.H. Hermann was published in the Financial Times on January 8, 1981. The article is attached as Appendix 9.

To have an interest in a practical topic is one thing, to research it and to write about it is another. Without the excellent group of national rapporteurs this Report would not have been realised. I am particularly happy that such concise and thorough reports have been submitted for those countries which have extensive and strongly enforced antitrust laws. It was the intention to add the national reports for the USA, EEC and Germany to the General Report, but for technical reasons it has only been possible to add the EEC report.

For those countries for which contributions have been made, developments up to December 1980 have been taken into account.

My time in private practice would have been far too limited to write the General Report alone. In Amanda Dalton I found a colleague who helped me with great knowledge and creativity.

Although no national reports were received on the Canadian and Dutch situations, a Canadian bill proposing blocking legislation is attached as Appendix 5 and a short description of the blocking legislation in the Netherlands is included in the General Report (under Point 10.3.9).

I regret that the legal situation in one major Western nation of growing importance, Japan, should not be included in this Report. As the topic of the enforcement of antitrust law outside national boundaries is here to stay and is a subject which will become even more important in the future, I hope that it will be possible to up-date this Report in a couple of years' time and that a chapter on the Japanese legal situation may then be included.

It is my hope that this Report may provide some guidance and assurance to all those confronted with antitrust problems with international implications.

*Cornelis Canenbley*

Düsseldorf, March 9, 1981

# Index

# 1. Brief outline of substantive law provisions

## 1.0 INTRODUCTION

The object of this report is not to deal with the material essence of substantive law as far as questions of extraterritoriality are concerned, but with procedural problems which arise when it is sought to apply and enforce national antitrust laws outside the territory of a state.

To place these procedures in context, it is proposed to outline briefly the nature of antitrust provisions within the various jurisdictions under discussion.

## 1.1 USA

The essentials of the U.S. antitrust system are to be found in three statutes: The Sherman Act, 15 USC §§ 1-7 (enacted in 1890), the Clayton Act, 15 USC §§ 12, 13, 14-21, 22-27 (also codified in scattered sections of 18, 29 USC) (enacted in 1914) and the Federal Trade Commission Act, 15 USC §§ 41-46, 47-58 (enacted in 1914) ('FTCA'). These statutes are supplemented by other minor acts and have themselves been amended in important ways, but collectively they provide the framework of U.S. antitrust control.

The Sherman Act prohibits '[e]very contract, combination in the form of trust or otherwise, or conspiracy, in restraint of trade' (Section 1). It is also directed at '[e]very person who shall monopolise, or attempt to monopolise, or combine or conspire with any other person or persons, to monopolise ...' (Section 2). Criminal offences are created, punishable by fines or imprisonment, and policed under the direction of the Department of Justice. Also provided for are proceedings akin to administrative proceedings – proceedings in equity to prevent and restrain violations of the law.

Responsibility for enforcement of the provisions of the Clayton Act is shared: the Department of Justice is empowered to institute civil proceedings under the Act, in addition, the Federal Trade Commission ('FTC') may investigate and issue 'cease and desist' orders against violations of the Act. Similarly, the FTCA does not create criminal offences, but charges the FTC with securing compliance with a general bar on 'unfair methods of competition'.

The antitrust provisions of U.S. law provide a system for control and review by the courts of monopolisation, of mergers (horizontal, vertical and conglomerate), and of restraint of trade arising from agreement or combination. The procedures available are civil actions, criminal procedures and 'administrative' proceedings.

## 1.2 GERMANY

The Gesetz gegen Wettbewerbsbeschränkungen ('GWB') contains the provisions of German antitrust law. Paragraph 1 GWB prohibits cartel agreements and declares them ineffective: this applies basically to horizontal agreements. Certain vertical agreements are also prohibited or subject to an abuse control by the cartel authority, Bundeskartellamt (BKartA): these cases are covered by paragraph 15 GWB and include attempts to influence the prices and conditions of one's customers (except with regard to books and similar press products).

Abuse of a dominant position on a market is subject to control under paragraph 22 GWB, which control is excercised by the BKartA. There are provisions for non-discrimination, in particular, paragraph 26 sub paragraph 2 GWB.

Mergers are subject to a system of notification to the BKartA, and the BKartA must prohibit a merger if it results in or strengthens a position of market domination (paragraph 24 GWB). Various presumptions as to market domination apply, and these have been broadened by a recent amendment to the GWB, made in April 1980.

The administration of the GWB is in the hands of the Bundeskartellamt which operates a system of notification and control similar in principle to that of the E.C. Commission. Two types of enforcement proceedings are available:

1. the administrative procedure (BKartA may issue a decision ordering or permitting certain behaviour);
2. the administrative fine procedure (BKartA may impose fines for violations of duties imposed by the GWB or of duties imposed by orders of the BKartA).

## 1.3 EEC

The substantive antitrust provisions of the EEC Treaty are Articles 85 and 86. These are directed at anticompetitive 'agreements between undertakings, decisions by associations of undertakings and concerted practices which may affect trade between member states' and at the abuse of a dominant position within the common market or a substantial part of it 'insofar as it may affect trade between member states' respectively. Regulation 17 of 1962 is the main implementing provision, and provides for a system of notification and review by the E.C. Commission of agreements, decisions and practices of the kind described in Art. 85(1) of the Treaty. Investigative powers vested in the Commission under Reg. 17/62 enable it also to act against infringements of Art. 86 EEC, (Art. 3 Reg. 17/62). Briefly, EEC law acts against restrictive agreements (Art. 85 EEC) and abuse of a dominant position (Art. 86 EEC). There is no provision for merger control as such. A proposal of the Commission to fill this gap has been pending before the Council of Ministers since 1973, but has not yet been adopted. However, in two areas the Commission – partly backed by the Court – has applied:

- Article 86 to certain mergers;
- Article 85 to certain concentrative joint ventures.

Under the provisions of Reg. 17/62 the E.C. Commission may make two types of Decision in cases of infringement of Article 85 or 86 EEC:

- cease and desist orders (Art. 3, Reg. 17/62);
- fine imposing Decisions (Art. 15, Reg. 17/62).

Decisions made under Reg. 17/62 are, however, stated not to be of a criminal law nature (Art. 15 (4), Reg. 17/62).

## 1.4 FRANCE

Under Art. 50 of the Ordonnance 45/1483 of 30/6/1945, concerted practices, contracts, express or tacit agreements or coalitions of whatever kind, and for whatever reason, which have as their object or effect the prevention, restriction or distortion of competition are prohibited.

The interference with normal market mechanisms by enterprises in a dominant position is also prohibited by Art. 50.

Art. 51 of the Ordonnance 45/1483 authorises such agreements and dominant positions when they are either expressly authorised by the law or when they ensure the promotion of economic progress.

A particular feature of proceedings under Art. 50 is that these may be either administrative or criminal proceedings. The Minister for the Economy may elect on the basis of an opinion given by the Commission de la Concurrence either to impose administrative fines or to transfer the case to the criminal jurisdiction. The transfer to the criminal jurisdiction is made in cases of very serious infringements. In administrative proceedings, appeal against the decision of the Minister can be made to the Conseil d'Etat.

The French Criminal Code, in Art. 419, creates various criminal offences, again by the categorisation of various activities upon the market; in essence it is directed against price fixing.

There is provision in the Loi of 19 July 1977 for a method of merger control where a merger may have an 'adverse effect' on competition. This control is of an administrative nature. In this respect the Loi provides for such control only when the joint turnover of the undertakings involved exceeds 40% of the national consumption when the products or services are of similar nature, or exceeds 25% of the national consumption when the products or services are of a different nature.

Notification of mergers is optional for the parties but the Minister for the Economy has power to ask the Commission de la Concurrence to direct investigations. On the basis of the Report of the Commission de la Concurrence the Minister may order that the project be stopped, or modified, or may order divestiture. The decision of the Minister is subject to appeal to the Conseil d'Etat.

The Loi of 19 July 1977 extends to total and partial concentrations and to joint ventures.

## 1.5 U.K.

The Restrictive Trade Practices Act 1976, which is a technical and complicated statute, applies in broad terms to agreements between two or more parties carrying on business in the United Kingdom in the production or supply of goods or the supply of services under which restrictions are accepted by two or more parties in respect of any of the matters specified in section 6 (in the case of goods) or section 9 (in the case of services) of the Act.

If an agreement is registrable, the whole of its terms whether or not relating to the restrictions which make it registrable, have to be furnished to the Director General of Fair Trading ('DGFT'). Insofar as the terms are recorded in writing, copies of all the documents are required; if any of the terms of the agreements are not in writing, a memorandum of those terms has to be furnished to the Director General. Except in the most exceptional circumstances, the agreement, when registered, is placed on a public register. The Director General has a duty to bring all agreements which are placed on the register before the Restrictive Practices Court for a decision as to whether or not the restrictions may be expected to operate against the public interest. The criteria to be used by the Court are laid down in the Act. They are onerous and difficult to satisfy. The burden of proof is upon the parties to the agreement to establish to the satisfaction of the Court that the agreement is in the public interest, failing which it will be condemned.

If the particulars of any agreement which is subject to registration are not furnished to the Director General before the restrictions take effect and within the time limit specified, there are two principal consequences: –

(a) The agreement is void in respect of those restrictions accepted under the agreement which made it registrable; and

(b) It is unlawful for any person who is a party to the agreement to give effect to or to enforce or purport to enforce those restrictions.

Monopoloy and merger control is provided for in the Fair Trading Act 1973. 'Monopoly situations' as defined in the Act are referable to the Monopolies and Mergers Commission (MMC) by the DGFT or the Secretary of State. The MMC must then report on the situation within a prescribed time limit, whereupon the Secretary of State may remedy any adverse effects of the monopoly by exercise of the wide powers conferred on him by the Act. Mergers (again subject to definition by the Act) may also be referred to the MMC for investigation. The Secretary of State may prohibit the merger, or order various actions by the undertakings concerned to protect the public interest. Prior notification of mergers to the DGFT is not required under U.K. law.

Control of 'anti-competitive practices' has been introduced by the Competition Act 1980. By section 2(1) of this Act: 'A person engages in an anti-competitive practice if, in the course of business, that person pursues a course of conduct which of itself or when taken together with a course of conduct pursued by persons associated with him, has or is intended to have or is likely to have the effect of restricting, distorting or preventing competition in connection with the production, supply or acquisition of goods in the United Kingdom or any part of it or the supply or securing of services in the United Kingdom or any part of it.'

## 1.6 SWITZERLAND

The Swiss antitrust legislation is built on the premise that cartel agreements or similar organisations are admissible as a matter of principle and provides relief only against certain qualified forms of abuse. Private actions are the forum in which the balancing of economic interests involved in determining abuses is carried out – there is no enforcement agency of the state to police freedom of competition.

The only enforceable public law remedy against a cartel is the so-called 'administrative action' filed by the Federal Economic Department. To date no such action has been filed.

## 1.7 ITALY

Italy has no national antitrust legislation other than that contained in the EEC provisions referred to previously. In the past thirty years, several antitrust Bills have been submitted for the approval of Parliament, but none has been adopted. No such Bills are pending.

## 1.8 AUSTRALIA

The major antitrust law provisions in Australia are contained in the Trade Practices Act 1974, since then significantly amended.

Part IV of this Act prohibits certain practices including:

(i) Contracts arrangements or undertakings restricting dealings or affecting competition or containing exclusion provisions (Section 45);

(ii) Contracts which have or are likely to have the effect of substantially lessening competition by price fixing for goods or services;

(iii) Boycotts by persons of the goods or services of other persons, where such boycotts would have the likely effect of causing a substantial loss or damage to the business (Section 45D);

(iv) A corporation, being in a position to control a market for goods, using its advantage to eliminate or substantially damage a person being a competitor in that market (Section 46);

(v) A corporation engaging in exclusive dealing for the supply of goods or services (Section 47);

(vi) Resale price maintenance or price discrimination (Section 48 and 49);

(vii) Under Part V of the Act, a corporation engaging in conduct that is misleading or deceptive or is likely to mislead or deceive (Section 52).

There are other provisions which relate to protection of consumers in Part V of the Act.

Should a person or corporation be guilty of a breach of Part IV or V the Commission, or the Minister, or any other person may seek an injunction restraining them from proceeding with such conduct (Section 80). There is an exception contained in this Act, but this exception does not warrant a further mention.

If a person has suffered loss by reason of a contravention by some person or corporation of Part IV or V of the Act, the amount of the loss can be recovered (Section 82). Criminal actions do not lie against the contravention of Part IV of the Act; however, the Court can fine any person who contravenes that Part up to $50,000 or, in the case of a corporation, up to $250,000.

An offence against Part V of the Act renders an individual liable to a fine of $10,000 and $50,000 in the case of a corporation. These fines are in addition to the injunction power previously referred to.

All actions in this regard must be taken before the Federal Court of Australia as this is a Court with jurisdiction.

The Trade Practices Commission is the body (established under the 1974 Act) responsible for the enforcement of the Trade Practices Act provisions. It is charged with the bringing of prosecutions before the Federal Court.

Under Section 88 of the Act, where the Commission is satisfied that certain proposed conduct would result or be likely to result in such benefit to the public that a proposed contract should be allowed, 'The Commission may upon application ... grant an authorisation to the corporation – To make a contract or arrangement where a provision of the proposed contract ... would be or might be an exclusionary provision or would have the purpose of substantially lessening competition within the meaning of Section 45.'

# 2. Is there substantive provision under national law for the extraterritorial application of that law?

## 2.0 INTRODUCTION

For the national cartel authority seeking to attack a violation of antitrust laws, as for the lawyer either defending a client from allegations of participation in restrictive trade practices or seeking to attack an antitrust violation in a civil action, the first question must be whether the national law concerned is applicable to enterprises not present within the geographical territory of the State concerned, i.e., does the law of the State in question apply to enterprises situated beyond its geographical boundaries? National legal provisions vary widely in this respect, and it is also frequently necessary to look beyond the mere wording of the provision and to examine that State's attitude towards the assumption of extraterritorial jurisdiction generally in seeking an answer. Thus, for instance, although the new U.K. Competition Act of 1980 has potential extraterritorial application on its face, recent OFT practices and the consistent attitude of the U.K. Courts over many years leads one to doubt whether it will be applied so as to include such cases in practice.

## 2.1 USA

Each of the major antitrust statutes outlined above has application in its substantive provisions to 'commerce among the several States, or with foreign nations'. The statutes prohibit activities, rather than being directed at nationals alone.

The United States Government adopts a far reaching approach to the application of its antitrust laws, to encompass any activity having an actual, substantial or principal effect within U.S. territory and intended to have such effect. (*See*, e.g., Address by U.S. Attorney General Griffin B. Bell, American Bar Association Assembly Luncheon, in Chicago, (Aug. 8, 1977); Maw, *Extraterritorial Application of U.S. Antitrust Law – 1978*, 7(iii) Int'l Bus. Law 154.) The approach of some U.S. courts in recent cases, however, has been to apply not the pure 'effects doctrine' but rather a 'rule-of-reason' approach embodying conflicts of law principles as well as considerations of international comity. (*See* e.g., *Mannington Mills, Inc., v. Congoleum Corp.*, 595 F. 2d 1287 (3d Cir. 1979); *Timberlane Lumber Co. v. Bank of America*, 549 F. 2d 597 (9th Cir. 1976).)

## 2.2 GERMANY

German antitrust law is not limited on its terms to the activities of nationals within German boundaries. Indeed, in paragraph 98 sub paragraph 2 GWB there is a clear provision for the application of an 'effects' principle:

> 'This law shall apply to all restraints on competition which have effect within the territory in which this law applies, even if such effects are caused by actions taken outside such territory.'

Following the amendment of the GWB made in April 1980, paragraph 98 sub paragraph 2, sentence 2 GWB provides for the application of the principle of personal jurisdiction in the case of export cartels, which must be notified to the BKartA, see Appendix 7:

> 'This law is applicable also to export cartels in the meaning of paragraph 6 sub paragraph 1 to the extent to which undertakings having their seat within the territory to which this law applies are participating.'

This provision has been introduced in order to enable the BKartA to control export cartels without having to prove that the activities of such cartels have effects upon the German market.

Paragraph 98 sub paragraph 2 GWB must, however, be read subject to Art. 25 G.G. (Grundgesetz), which makes general rules of public international law part of the federal legal system and allows them to enjoy ascendancy over German laws and to produce immediate rights and duties for the German people. Thus paragraph 98 sub paragraph 2 GWB can take effect only insofar as it is in conformity with general principles of international law.

Although, hitherto, it was difficult to detect an official tendency or policy with regard to the extraterritorial application of German antitrust law, it may be said that the BKartA has been reluctant to apply antitrust provisions about cartels, abuse of a dominant position etc. to foreign enterprises. Recently, however, the BKartA has penalised foreign companies for their participation in a cartel which had effects within Germany (*Casting, Roller* case, of Press Release of the BKartA 16/80 of September 1st, 1980).

Such reluctance is not evident in the policy of the BKartA in the field of merger control. The BKartA has interpreted paragraph 98 sub paragraph 2 GWB to mean that mergers which are effected completely abroad but which have an appreciable effect upon the German market are subject to merger control. (For further details see BKartA's guidelines to the domestic impact of mergers in the meaning of paragraph 98 sub paragraph 2 GWB, Appendix 6.)

In one actual case the BKartA prohibited a merger which was completely effected abroad (acquisition of the assets of Firestone France by the French subsidiary of Bayer, Germany cf. FAZ September 30, 1980; Handelsblatt October 1, 1980). According to the BKartA Bayer had a dominating position on the German market in synthetic rubber and had strengthened this position by acquiring Firestone France which produced synthetic rubber but also sold only 2% of its production on the German market (the rest sold mainly in France).

The Appellate Court of Berlin (Kammergericht) annulled the BKartA's decision (cf. Handelsblatt November 27, 1980) for the following reasons:

– The decision was not served on the US parent of Firestone France.

– The right to be heard had not been granted to Firestone, France nor Firestone, USA before the issuance of the prohibition order.

– The decision was not sufficiently founded. The Appellate Court granted Bayer the right to consummate the acquisition.

Further, the Court directed that the German authorities in their examination of whether a merger completely effected abroad produces appreciable effects within Germany must take into consideration the interests of foreign states involved and must give reasons in their decision as to why the balancing of German interests against the interests of foreign states requires the application of German law. Although the Court agreed with the legal evaluation of the BKartA that Bayer had a market dominating position on the German market for synthetic rubber and that this market dominating position was strengthened by Bayer's acquisition of Firestone's French production plant and that therefore all requirements for a prohibition order under German law were given, the Appellate Court held that the application of German merger control law was overruled by international law for the following specific reasons:

– The participating companies (Bayer, France and Firestone, France) were foreign companies.

– The acquired assets (production plant) were located outside Germany.

– Only a small part of the production of the foreign plant was sold on the German market.

## 2.3 EEC

The major criterion for the application of EEC antitrust provisions is the affecting of trade between Member States. This may be satisfied by enterprises outside the geographical jurisdiction of the EEC as well as by those situated within it. It is worth mentioning that the European Court of Justice has not yet applied the 'effects doctrine', but in the only case in which it had an opportunity to express a view, (the Dyestuffs cases, Cases 48/69, 52/69 and 53/69, ICI, Geigy, Sandoz; 1972 ECR, 619, 787, 845), it stressed both that the anticompetitive behaviour *took place* partly within the EEC and *had an effect* upon competition within the territory of the EEC.

## 2.4 FRANCE

The criterion for the application of French antitrust law is the effect on the French market.

The substantive provisions of the Ordonnance 45/1483 and Art. 419 of the Penal Code are prima facie applicable to foreign enterprises outside the jurisdiction. (i.e. Opinion of the Commission Technique des Ententes in: *Electric Lamps Industry* 26.5.1976 and 22.4.1966, J.O. 1193-67 p. 34 and 1193-69 p. 9; *Stoneware Industry*: 21.9.1973, J.O. Doc. Adm. No. 66 of 19.7.1974 p. 2614).

As these are penal provisions, Art. 693 of the Code of Criminal Procedure applies which provides that where one of the constituent elements of an offence has been effected in France, that offence is considered to have been committed within French territory.

At least some authors consider that French antitrust provisions might be applicable to foreign enterprises outside the jurisdiction on the basis of the 'objective territoriality' theory, by which a criminal law is capable of application by the jurisdictions of a state when an infringement has direct effects within the territory of that state. (Goldman – 'Les champs d'application des lois sur la concurrence', Rec. Cours. Acad. Droit International 1969.)

2.5 U.K.

The Restrictive Trade Practices Act prohibitions apply only as between 'two or more persons carrying on business in the U.K.' or their trade association. A person is not deemed to carry on business within the U.K. by reason only of the fact that he is represented for the purpose of that business by an agent within the U.K. Thus this statute has only very limited potential for extra-territorial application. Also, the Restrictive Practices Court may make orders only against parties to an agreement 'who carry on a business within the U.K.' or their trade association.

The Anti-Competitive Practices (Exclusions) Order (S.I. 1980 No. 979) of 14 July 1980 starts its list of 'excluded courses of conduct' in Schedule 1 para 1. (i.e. conduct which is not to be treated as anti-competitive under the Competition Act 1980) with the words: 'Any course of conduct which consists of – (a) the inclusion in contracts for the supply of goods of conditions relating solely to the supply of those goods outside the United Kingdom, or (b) the refusal to supply goods upon such conditions.'

Monopoly situations are defined with regard to goods and services supplied in the U.K. and in the case of monopolies regarding exports, to goods produced in the U.K. Merger situations are defined with regard to two or more enterprises one of which, at least, was carried on in the U.K., or by or under the control of a body corporate incorporated in the U.K. ceasing to be distinct enterprises. (FTA 1973). Here, therefore, there is limited scope for extra-territorial application, but, in circumstances where foreign enterprises are involved, the enquiries of the DGFT or MMC are usually directed within the U.K.

Section 90(3) FTA provides that nothing in any governmental order under ss 56, 73, 74 or 89 (re mergers) 'shall have effect so as to apply to any person in relation to his conduct outside the United Kingdom' unless that person is a U.K. citizen or company or carries on business in the U.K.

The U.K. Government has shown itself very hostile to attempted assertions of extraterritorial jurisdiction in antitrust matters by other states. It has passed 'blocking' legislation upon a number of occasions and protested in the strongest possible terms (*See* e.g. Aide Memoire to the E.C. Commission concerning the Dyestuffs case, in 1972). Thus, it is only reasonable to assume that extraterritorial jurisdiction will not be asserted by U.K. courts, and past practice reflects this view.

## 2.6 SWITZERLAND

In the case of antitrust legislation, the Federal Court has made it clear that the attitude of Swiss law towards an extraterritorial application of rules ultimately serving the protection of the Swiss economic order will be very reserved. (*See* e.g. the *Hachette* case, OECD Guide to Legislation on Restrictive Business Practises, Vol. I, Switzerland, section 3.0, p. 5.)

## 2.7 ITALY

Not applicable.

## 2.8 AUSTRALIA

The general principle applied to all Australian legislation is that it is presumed to be limited territorially, and there is a requirement that there be evidence of express intention in any statute prior to its being held capable of extraterritorial application.

The Trade Practices Act, 1974 (as amended) contains several sections which specifically extend the power of the Act to extraterritorial situations. The Act is based primarily on Section 51 (XX) of the Constitution which is commonly called 'the corporations power'. A foreign corporation or a trading and financial corporation must be involved.

The definitions of these corporations are contained in the Trade Practices Act which in its definition of 'corporation' refers back to a 'corporation within the meaning of Section 51 (XX) of the Constitution' and includes, in the case of a foreign corporation, 'a body corporate which is incorporated in an external territory'. Also relevant as a constituting power is Section 51(1), the trade and commerce power, and also the external affairs' power.

In view of the purposes of the Act and references to foreign corporations, it would appear that the legislature expressly intended the Act to have extraterritorial application, although possibly limited to specific areas.

# 3. Relevant principles of international law

## 3.1 THE PRINCIPLE OF STATE SOVEREIGNTY

According to this principle, each State is the sole arbiter of the legal nature of acts performed within its territory. Only the public authorities of that State have the right to act within the territory. Thus an act of public authority of State A performed within the territory of State B, is an infringement of the Sovereignty of State B, unless previously consented to by the government or other designated authority of State B.

There are well recognised exceptions to this principle, developed in state practice over many years, whereby, for example, a state is regarded as competent under international law to punish aliens for acts done abroad which are directly connected with a crime within its territory. Crimes such as murder fall within this exception, which is, however, generally held to be applicable only to those crimes which all civilised nations condemn. Crimes of an economic nature, such as those existing in various jurisdictions in antitrust provisions, are not traditionally numbered amongst these exceptional cases, for the policy of one state in this area may differ greatly from that of another.

It should further be recognised that the definition of 'an act of public authority' may be different in different national jurisdictions. With regard to the permissibility of service abroad, for example, the issue is not whether the document to be served may carry penalties (whether it is coercive) but whether it is a document issuing from a public authority of the state from which service is issuing. 'Public authority' in this context certainly embraces traditional executive, legislative and judicial bodies. Whether a private lawyer is to be seen as a 'public authority' or as an agent of such is open to debate. An American lawyer, conducting a deposition abroad, without judicial supervision, in pre-trial discovery proceedings, might well fall outside such a definition. Once the power of a court has been invoked and process is served, certainly an act of public authority is involved.

It is important to retain the distinction between the decision or document to be served and the act of service of that decision. Similarly, delivery as a factual event and service as a legal procedure may be distinguished and thus it may be argued that the sending of simple letters, i.e. the mere use of foreign postal officials, is not to be seen as the official act of the issuing foreign office.

Thus, there seems to be general consensus among the States which are examined here on the question of the legality under international law of informal inquiries directed at an enterprise outside the territorial jurisdiction. Such informal requests for information, made by ordinary mail, telephone or telex, are regarded as in conformity with international law with regard to the issue of state sovereignty. Some commentators see this as resulting from the non-coercive nature of such inquiries (EEC), while the majority derive their conclusion from the unofficial nature of the request. (Germany, U.K., USA)

Two exceptions to this general consensus of opinion must be noted: According to the Swiss Federal Department of Justice and Police, letters of a foreign authority addressed to a Swiss resident are regarded as an interference with Swiss sovereignty and the act of sending them is punishable under Art. 271 of the Swiss Penal Code.

According to the French Loi of 16 July 1980 (Art ler bis) it is forbidden for any person to ask, by writing, orally or in any form whatsoever, for any document or information of economic, commercial, industrial, financial or technical nature and to communicate these documents when they are such as to tend to constitute evidence for foreign proceedings, either judicial or administrative.

This law is criminal in nature, but is, however, not applicable when there exists an international convention authorising such communication.

## 3.2 THE INTERNATIONAL LAW PRINCIPLE OF COMITY

This principle has been variously defined but is clearly recognised to exist by all international law writers. Brownlie has described it as involving 'neighbourliness, mutual respect and the friendly waiver of technicalities.' The operation of the principle is perhaps well illustrated in the handling of letters rogatory by the courts. In the *Westinghouse Case*, Lord Denning, in the Court of Appeal, expressed the principle as follows:

> 'Such is the request made by the United States Federal Court. It is our duty and our pleasure to do all we can to assist that court, just as we would expect the United States court to help us in like circumstances. Do unto others as you would be done by.'

Under this principle, nations are under a moral duty to cooperate with each other in enforcing their respective laws, and to resolve international conflicts fairly with a sensitivity to each other's interests.

## 3.3 THE RIGHT TO BE HEARD IN YOUR OWN DEFENCE

This right is a fundamental human right and probably has sufficient support in observance by State practice to have the status of a customary rule of international law. It can be argued that the right to be heard would be violated by the public service of process within the jurisdiction upon a party outside the jurisdiction. A counter argument is that there is no problem unless an abuse of law is involved, for example, if such a time for public service is chosen as is known to be difficult or inconvenient for the foreign enterprise involved. The international law requirement of the guarantee of a fair trial is also involved here – the complainant must have an opportunity to know the extent of the complaint against him.

## 3.4 JURISDICTION BASED UPON NATIONALITY; PERSONAL JURISDICTION

Under U.S. law, a corrective to the potentially wide-reaching extraterritorial application of substantive antitrust law is found by the courts in the requirement that they have 'personal jurisdiction' over the parties brought before them. This requirement will be discussed further under Point 3.5 below.

What is at issue is the extent to which a State, even one which takes a strictly territorial view with respect to the application of its antitrust law, may still reserve for itself the right to apply certain of its laws to its own nationals, wherever they may be found. One procedural illustration of this attitude is found in the area of service of process abroad, where many States will serve process upon their own nationals directly through consular or diplomatic officials without notifying the authorities of the host State, and without objecting to similar procedure being followed by consular staff of other nations present upon their own territory.

Nationality, as an aspect of sovereignty and a mark of allegiance, is generally recognised as a basis for jurisdiction over extraterritorial acts. The application of the principle may be extended by reliance upon residence and other connections (as evidence of allegiance owed by aliens), (*see* e.g. *Nottebohm* decision of the International Court of Justice ([1955] ICJ 4 ), and also by ignoring changes of nationality. (*See* Point 3.5 below). The potential for the creation of parallel jurisdiction, and hence, double jeopardy, due to the incidence of dual nationality and conflicts between the territoriality and nationality principles creating jurisdiction, has led many States to place limitations upon the nationality principle as a basis for jurisdiction, and it is often confined to serious offences.

### 3.4.1 USA

Under American law the courts have the power to order individuals and entities over whom they have personal jurisdiction to do or to refrain from doing acts outside the U.S. The scope of such orders is circumscribed by the limits of substantive jurisdiction. In other words, the order is limited to conduct that has or would have the requisite effect upon U.S. foreign commerce.

In upholding the constitutionality of a statute (28 USC § 1783) under which subpoenas might be issued to witnesses in foreign countries in order to compel testimony or production of documents, either for discovery or for trial, where the individuals are either citizens of the U.S. or residents thereof the Supreme Court stated in *Blackmer* v. *United States*, 284 U.S. 421, 437 (1932) that:

'... the United States possesses the power inherent in sovereignty to require the return to this country of a citizen, resident elsewhere, whenever the public interest requires it, and to penalise him in case of refusal...'

The reasoning is that the U.S. still retains *in personam* jurisdiction over its non-resident citizens. This form of jurisdiction also allows the issuance of subpoenas to aliens who are at the moment in a foreign country but who reside in the U.S. (*See* Point 5 below).

United States courts have also issued orders compelling non-resident aliens to take or to refrain from taking specified actions outside U.S. territory. These orders have included: injunctions against acts that would violate U.S. antitrust laws, orders requiring divestiture of stockholdings in foreign corporations, transfer of foreign patent and trademark rights, reasonable efforts to promote the sale and distribution of products in foreign countries, and orders instructing alien defendants to amend an agreement made in a foreign country. (*See*, e.g., *United States* v. *Imperial Chemical Industries Ltd.*, 105 F. Supp. 215 (SDNY 1952) (the 'ICI' case); *United States* v. *National Lead Co.*, 332 U.S. 319 (1947); *United States* v. *Watchmakers of Switzerland Information Centre Inc.* Civ. No. 90-170, at 14 (SDNY, Order of Jan 22, 1964).)

### 3.4.2 Germany

In the application of the principle of effect according to paragraph 98 sub paragraph 2 GWB, the BKartA has the power to order that German residents have to cease and desist from any acts outside Germany, which may have adverse effects within Germany. This power has been exercised with regard to mergers (prohibition of merger between a foreign and a German enterprise, GKN/Sachs case WuW/E BKartA 1625), participation by German enterprises in international cartels and restrictive licensing agreements between German licensors and foreign licensees. (*See* e.g. the *Oil-Field-Tube Case* 1973 WuW/E BGH 1276)

### 3.4.3 EEC

The question of exercising jurisdiction appears to have been decided almost exclusively on a substantive law basis (*see* however Point 3.5 below).

### 3.4.4 France

There exists no special provision whereby the French antitrust authorities have power to order French residents to do or refrain from doing acts outside the territorial boundaries. However, in the case of administrative proceedings and insofar as the acts in question have effects within French territory, it is possible that the Minister for the Economy (on the basis of an Opinion of the Commission de la Concurrence) might order a French resident to do or to refrain from doing such acts outside the territorial boundaries.

### 3.4.5 U.K.

U.K. antitrust authorities may order U.K. residents to do or refrain from doing acts outside U.K. territory only in so far as those acts relate to the carrying on of a business within the U.K. in the production or supply of goods or the supply of services (RTPA 1976 ss 6 (1), 9 (1) and 35 (4)).

### 3.4.6 Switzerland

Neither the present cartel law nor the draft revision confer powers on the Swiss administrative authorities or courts in connection with the application of the law to order a person resident in Switzerland with respect to conduct abroad. This reflects Switzerland's defensive attitude towards attempts by foreign authorities to apply their administrative laws, antitrust or other, in Switzerland.

### 3.4.7 Italy

Not applicable.

### 3.4.8 Australia

The Trade Practices Commission has no power to order a resident to do or refrain from doing any act outside the jurisdiction.

Under the 'Foreign Proceedings (Prohibition of Certain Evidence) Act' of 1976, the Attorney General was given very wide powers, inter alia, that to 'by an order in writing prohibit ... the giving by a person at a time when he is an Australian citizen or is a resident of Australia, of evidence before a foreign tribunal in relation to, or to the contents of, documents that at the time of the making of the order were or at any time while the order is in force are in Australia'. Service of such an order may be made publicly, in the Government Gazette, personally, or by post. This act was assented to on 15 March 1979.

An Order was issued by the Attorney General, under this Act, prohibiting persons from giving evidence about documents in Australia in the *Westinghouse Case*.

## 3.5 STATE HOSPITALITY TO COMMERCE

There may exist a principle of international law of uncertain scope whereby enterprises to whom hospitality is afforded for their commerce by a State are under a duty to conform to the laws of that State. This principle, which may be called the principle of sovereign hospitality, is particularly noteworthy in the development of the notion of personal jurisdiction in the United States.

### 3.5.1 USA

Assertions of personal jurisdiction have enabled U.S. courts to extend their jurisdiction to cover activities of foreign enterprises having some sufficient contact with the United States. Such enterprises are regarded as under a duty to conform with United States antitrust law by reason of their acceptance of U.S. State hospitality for their commerce.

What constitutes a sufficient contact to found personal jurisdiction (in this context) is uncertain. The traditional statement of the test as expressed in *International Shoe Co.* v. *Washington*, 326 U.S. 310, 316 (1945) (quoting *Milliken* v. *Meyer*, 311 U.S. 457, 463 (1940)), is whether a defendant has contacts with the forum of such a nature and quality that the maintenance of the suit does not offend 'traditional (American) notions of fair play and substantial justice'. Foreign enterprises engaged in active trade on the American market in the supply or production of goods or services would obviously be included, as would those with some office or production facilities on United States territory. It would also appear that one who seeks the grant of United States patents for his inventions can have no complaint if the grantor insists that the patentee abide by the terms of its statutes and be subject to the normal penalties for misuse of the grant, as is illustrated by *United States* v. *Imperial Chemical Industries Ltd.*, 105 F. Supp. 215 (SDNY 1952). In the recent case of *World-Wide Volkswagen Corp.* v. *Woodson*, 100 S. Ct. 559 (1980), it was held by the Supreme Court that a German producer and his major distributor could be sued in any state of the United States on a product liability suit, on the grounds that any such firm having set up a distribution and service network must expect that consumers might purchase their goods in any state. Thus it may be seen that this principle will be broadly applied to justify the extension of jurisdiction of United States Courts. The 'minimum contacts' test is not susceptible to mechanical application, rather various factors must be weighed. The factors include: continuous activities of agents, business volume, meetings, banking, business correspondence, and employment of local personnel. (*See*, e.g. *Wells Fargo & Co.* v. *Wells Fargo Express Co.*, 556 F, 2d 406 (9th Cir. 1977): *PSC Corp.* v. *Toshiba America, Inc.*, 491 F 2d 1064 (9th Cir. 1974).

### 3.5.2 EEC

In some cases the Commission has apparently taken the position that enterprises located outside the EEC submit themselves to the jurisdiction of the Commission by filing the agreement with the Commission or even only by consenting that their participation in the agreement be mentioned in the application for a negative clearance or an exemption. There is, however, no consistent approach either by the Commission or by the European Court of Justice to this question at the present time.

Assuming substantive jurisdiction, based on the effects doctrine, it is unclear what role a jurisdictional rule of procedure based on personal jurisdiction might play. This is not a point that has ever been examined by the European Court of Justice, although it was available for discussion in the United Brands Decision ('Chiquita' Case 27/67; 1978 ECR 207). The Court has not gone into the argument here, contenting itself with use of the enterprise entity doctrine to facilitate the grounding of substantive jurisdiction.

### 3.5.3 Germany

By contrast to United States antitrust procedure, German law knows no notion of personal jurisdiction. However, in the majority of cases appreciable 'effects' within the jurisdiction will only be caused by such enterprises as have continuous and substantial business within the meaning of the condition of personal jurisdiction in United States antitrust law. In the case of export cartels paragraph 98, sub paragraph 2, sentence 2, GWC as amended in April 1980, provides for the application of German anti-trust law if German enterprises are participating, regardless of whether the export cartel produces effects within Germany.

### 3.5.4 Switzerland

The physical presence within the jurisdiction constitutes the relevant point of attachment to justify the assumption of jurisdiction for the opening of administrative procedures under Swiss law. There is no notion of personal jurisdiction in the sense in which this arises in United States law. Criteria of presence within the jurisdiction, or of being 'found' or 'transacting business' are irrelevant for the jurisdictional issue.

**Final remark:**

These instances illustrate one major problem of extraterritorial procedure; some systems appear to rely upon the same criteria for founding jurisdiction both in substantive and procedural antitrust law (e.g. Switzerland, France), whereas other legal systems divide the two, as in United States law. Thus far in its evolution, EEC law seems uncertain about the adoption of this distinction.

# 4. National procedural rules

## 4.0 INTRODUCTION

Upon the assumption that there is substantive jurisdiction under national law over the foreign enterprise abroad, the next question for the civil suitor or administrative body anxious to institute proceedings must be whether national rules of procedure provide for the furtherance of proceedings against such an enterprise.

Various issues arise here. It may be desirable to obtain from abroad further evidence in the form of documents or testimony of witnesses for use at the projected trial. It will usually be necessary, especially where administrative offences are involved, for decisions of the cartel authorities to be formally notified to the defendant (*see* e.g. Germany, EEC), and where it is decided to pursue the issue in the courts, it will be necessary for process to be served. Finally, the effectiveness of national antitrust policy must depend upon the ability to put into practical effect the relief granted by the courts. Thus the enforcement of favourable judgments against foreign defendants is also a crucial issue.

Acts such as the gathering of pre-trial evidence and the service of process may be regarded as having a different legal nature in different legal systems. Few States would contest that the service of process is an act of public authority of the State whose courts are being called upon to exercise jurisdiction, and therefore the performance of such an act upon the territory of another State, without that State's permission or consent, would be an infringement of the sovereignty of that State. But what of pre-trial discovery procedures? American courts accept a very much broader availability of such discovery than do other jurisdictions. Also, under American law, much of the procedure for discovering and producing evidence is left to the parties. Generally, there is no prior judicial authorisation or control. By contrast, for example, in French civil or commercial actions evidence is only submitted in written form and procedures for oral evidence do not come into play unless the court considers the documents submitted by the parties to be inconclusive. 'At this stage control of the evidence gathering process passes from the parties to the judge, to whom the French Code of Civil Procedure grants broad and exclusive powers' (Code de Procedure Civile Tit. VII (Fr.); Judicial Administration of Evidence, Source: Jacques Borel, Stephen M. Boyd; 'International Lawyer', from ABA Annual Meeting in New York on Aug. 7, 1978). Whether an American Lawyer engaged in a spot of 'legal tourism'* in a civil law country

* A 'legal tourist' is an American lawyer who instals himself in a deluxe hotel room for as little as one day or as long as six weeks, with a degree of circumspection which demonstrates great deference to the

for the gathering of pre-trial evidence can be said to be improperly performing a public judicial act and thus infringing the foreign State's sovereignty, must be open to argument.

Clearly, much will depend upon the forum in which the issue will be discussed and where the issue falls in that legal system. An American court is unlikely to take arguments against subsequent production of such evidence based on an allegation of illegality against the methods used in obtaining it. (*See* e.g., In re; *Uranium Antitrust Litigation*, 480 F. Supp. 1138 (N.D. Ill. 1979). Presumably, the attitude of a French court within whose jurisdiction such an unsupervised deposition had been conducted would be very different.

The above discussion is designed to illustrate only that national rules of procedure develop as an integral part of the legal system which they serve, and tend towards the same political bias as shown by the substantive law aims which they are designed to facilitate within that system. In practice, the forum within which procedural issues of this nature are heard is bound always to be crucial.

It is proposed to commence with an examination of purely extraterritorial national procedures, in the strict sense of procedures which take effect outside the territorial boundaries of the state concerned, and to leave for subsequent examination other methods whereby a foreign enterprise may be brought within the jurisdiction of a national court for acts performed abroad, for example, by the application of the enterprise entity doctrine or by fastening upon an arm of the enterprise located within the territorial jurisdiction.

## 4.1 USA

### 4.1.1 Written requests for information (discovery orders)

Under the Antitrust Civil Process Act, 15 USC § 1311-1314 (enacted in 1962), the Antitrust Division of the Department of Justice has authority to issue 'civil investigative demands' ('CIDs') for the purpose of obtaining documentary material or oral testimony pertinent to antitrust investigations. Such a demand may be served upon a person not found within the territorial jurisdiction of any court of the United States, in such manner as the Federal Rules of Civil Procedure (Fed. R. Civ. P.) provide for service in a foreign country. Rule 4(i) Fed. R. Civ. P. is the relevant rule, and provides for a number of ways in which papers may be served in foreign countries, such as by mail, personal delivery, and in the manner prescribed by the law of the foreign country.

---

principle of professional confidentiality. Once installed, 'legal tourists' use their best efforts to obtain, primarily by means of depositions, the testimony of witnesses and the documents with which they hope successfully to represent the interests of their clients in a United States court. Citizens of France, the United States and third countries are invited unceremoniously to testify in what might irreverently be described as a three-star chamber.

The Antitrust Division has used this power, having advised the pertinent foreign authorities of their action, but, having encountered such reactions as the forbidding of the private parties involved to produce the requested documents, has now decided to proceed by seeking overseas discovery on a voluntary basis, *i.e.* with the acquiescence of both the foreign party and its government.

In a civil case, Rule 45 Fed. R. Civ. P. in conjunction with Section 1783 of the Judicial Code provides for the issuance of subpoenas to citizens or residents of the U.S. located abroad to compel appearance as a witness or for the production of documents. It must be shown that the evidence sought is necessary in the interests of justice and may not be obtained in any other manner.

### 4.1.2 Production and disclosure of documents located abroad

Apart from the provisions of the Antitrust Civil Process Act outlined above, United States federal courts consider that they have the authority to require the production of documents located abroad where the court has *in personam* jurisdiction over the person or entity in possession or control of the material. On the other hand, foreign law may pose an obstacle to the production of the documents located abroad. There have been many disputes in U.S. antitrust cases as to the obligations of the person served with the discovery order when he is thus caught between two sovereigns. The ruling of the court often turns on such factors as whether the foreign law is criminal or civil in nature and what the person has done in good faith to have the application of the foreign law lifted.

Two examples are used to illustrate how the appropriate resolution of this issue depends largely upon the particular facts and circumstances of each case.

In *Application of Chase Manhatten Bank*, 192 F. Supp, 817 (SDNY 1961), aff'd, 297 F 2d 611 (2d Cir. 1962), the Government was seeking to compel the bank, a New York corporation, to produce records in the possession of a branch located in the Republic of Panama. The bank presented expert evidence of a recent Panamanian enactment under which production of the records would constitute an offence equivalent to that of committing a misdemeanour under U.S. criminal law.

The district court concluded that production would constitute a violation of Panamanian law, and stayed any further enforcement proceedings. The government was left to petition the Panamanian Government directly for permission to obtain the records, but the subpoena was left outstanding against Chase, to ensure that it complied with its duty of co-operating with the Government in any petition to the foreign authorities.

In *United States v. First National City Bank*, 396 F 2d 897 (2d Cir. 1968), what was involved was not the threat of criminal sanctions which City Bank might incur by production of the information, but the fact that such production might leave it vulnerable to civil liability and economic loss. The issue was bank secrecy, the breach of which privilege owed to the customer could subject the bank to liability in contract or tort. The factors weighed by the Second Circuit were: the relative importance given to American antitrust law and German bank secrecy tradition in their respective jurisdictions; the absence of governmental concern in the matter; the unlikelihood of any action being brought to a successful conclusion by the customer concerned in the light of the defences available to City Bank and the consistent refusal of the customer to seek an injunction restraining production of the information by City Bank.

### 4.1.3 Search and investigation of persons or companies abroad

Other than as previously indicated, the antitrust authorities may not investigate outside the United States. They do interrogate persons abroad on a voluntary basis where both the persons concerned and the foreign government concerned have no objections. It is their policy to advise the foreign government before conducting the interview. Where the foreign government objects, the antitrust authorities are unlikely to pursue the investigation on foreign soil.

### 4.1.4 Hearing of defendants or witnesses abroad

A defendant or a witness may agree to a deposition being conducted outside the United States in connection with an antitrust proceeding. Both parties' counsel are entitled to be present at such a deposition to question the deponent. The deposition can then be used at the trial, subject to certain conditions. The statement of a defendant or witness outside the country can sometimes be presented by a sworn affidavit. The trial or the hearing of the case itself will, however, take place within the United States.

### 4.1.5 Service of process abroad

Under the terms of Rule 4 of the Federal Rules of Civil Procedure, service of process may be made in a foreign country pursuant to the terms of either an applicable federal statute or the State's 'long-arm' statute. The most important federal statute dealing with service of process in antitrust cases is Section 12 of the Clayton Act which provides that process may be served on a corporate defendant in antitrust cases where-ever it may be found. There are also 'long-arm' statutes in many States which provide for service of process on persons not found within the State. Accordingly, service of process in antitrust cases is usually easy to accomplish, even where service is to be effected in a foreign country.

Rule 4(1)(i) Fed. R. Civ. P. makes provision regarding the formality of service of process abroad.

### 4.1.6 Reactions of foreign governments

There have been many instances of the protest of foreign governments to the wide-reaching activities of United States antitrust authorities. This has led to a slight retrenchment, for example by the Antitrust Division of the Department of Justice, regarding the issue of discovery orders. It is now the policy of this Department to seek overseas discovery on a voluntary basis, that is, with the consent of both the foreign party and its government. A similar policy has been adopted with regard to the interrogation of persons abroad on a voluntary basis where both the persons concerned and the foreign government have no objection.

The real area of difficulty with regard to United States jurisdiction arises in pre-trial situations in civil suits, rather than in investigations conducted by the Justice Department. There is a fundamental difference between the American and other national systems for discovery and production of evidence before a court. Under American procedure the discovery and production of evidence is left primarily to the parties. Generally, there is no prior judicial authorisation or control, the role of the court being to enforce applicable rules, resolve procedural disputes, and protect against potential abuse. Thus, the conducting of depositions abroad will probably be the task of the attorney whose client is seeking compensation for damage inflicted by the operation of a cartel. Under American procedure, the conducting of such a deposition is not regarded as the exercise of State power. Other jurisdictions might, however, regard it as such and seek the aid of State officials to reject the authority of such an attorney on the basis of an infringement of jurisdiction.

It would be foolish to disregard the fact that a major objection to American procedural rules felt by parties from other national jurisdictions is that they entail great expense and are frequently drawn out over a very long period of time. The fact that the broad provisions for discovery under American procedure frequently result in the conducting of what are known as 'fishing expeditions' abroad is another cause for hostile reaction. To spend time and money complying with such discovery procedures without even the certainty that one is defending oneself against any concrete accusation but inadvertently may be laying oneself open to a subsequent civil suit, is bound to lead to an outraged sense of injustice.

## 4.2 GERMANY

Procedure in the enforcement of German antitrust law is considerably more conservative than in the United States. It is necessary for a proper understanding of extraterritorial procedural provisions to give a general outline of the procedure followed by antitrust authorities within national boundaries.

Two kinds of proceedings for the enforcement of antitrust law should be distinguished: (1) the administrative procedure, in which the cartel authorities may issue a decision ordering or giving permission for certain acts or behaviour; and (2) the administrative fine procedure, by which the cartel authorities may impose fines on enterprises in cases where the law specifically provides for such fines for violations of duties, whether imposed by the law itself or by orders of the cartel authorities.

### *1. Administrative Procedures*

The cartel authorities have discretion to open a procedure on their own initiative or based on a complaint. They possess broad powers of investigation, for the exercise of which, however, in certain cases they need the prior permission of a judge. These powers are only granted for the investigation of special cases, not for general inquiries. In particular, no 'fishing orders' without reference to specific circumstances may be issued. Orders for requests for information concerning the economic position of an enterprise and the inspection and examination of documents must be made by formal decision of the cartel authorities. It is customary to attempt to obtain this information by sending ordinary letters which are not formally served, but which contain the announcement that, in the case of refusal to furnish the information, a formal decision will be issued. In order to search the premises of an enterprise the formal permission of a judge with competent jurisdiction is needed.

The procedure followed here is in practice the same as that laid down for the E.C. Commission, in relation to requests for information under Article 11 of Regulation 17/62 i.e. involving a two-tier system whereby an informal request is followed by a formal request by way of decision.

As a matter of law, the cartel authorities have to grant due process to the person or enterprise affected, which, in particular, includes the right to be heard, which is one of the fundamental legal rights granted by the German constitution. To comply with this obligation, the cartel authorities write a letter summarising the results of the investigation, which is normally subject to formal service of process. Objections may be lodged within a certain period of time, after which the final decision is issued. This is also subject to formal service of process.

### *2. Administrative fine procedure*

The cartel authorities may initiate investigations of all kinds and ask all other authorities for information. They have the power to consult witnesses and experts, who have to appear before the office of the cartel authorities. Except in cases of special urgency, the cartel authorities may carry out searches and seizures only with the permission of a judge with competent jurisdiction. The person affected cannot be compelled to produce any documents, as this would be a violation of the constitutional right which provides that no person may be forced to incriminate himself. Any evidence may be seized only with the prior consent of a judge, save in cases of immediate danger and urgency. Where such a case arises, the documents seized must be submitted to the competent judge for approval within three days of seizure. Before the formal decision is issued the cartel authorities either have to grant the person affected a hearing or grant an opportunity for comment on the facts investigated and on the legal aspects of the case. This is usually done by letter. Such letters are subject to formal service of process. The decision itself has to be formally served on the person or company affected.

### 4.2.1 Written requests for information (discovery orders)

According to German legal theory, service of process constitutes an act of sovereignty and therefore falls under the general prohibition on such acts when performed outside the national territory. The German cartel authorities are thus not entitled to send any decisions or other acts which require formal service of process abroad without the prior consent and assistance of the authorities of the foreign State. The German cartel authorities have never tried to send formal decisions ordering information or discovery outside Germany and have never attempted to get the permission and assistance of foreign States for such measures. However, the posting of normal letters cannot be seen as a violation of sovereignty, and therefore the German cartel authorities in quite a number of cases have sent normal letters to foreign addressees in which foreign residents or companies have been asked to deliver information or documents voluntarily to the German cartel authorities. It appears that, in a number of cases, these letters have been sent without informing the authorities of the foreign state to which the letter was sent. In several such cases the foreign persons or enterprises have answered such letters.

### 4.2.2 Production and disclosure of documents located abroad

If the authorities receive no response to a request for information, as under 4.2.1 above, in administrative proceedings, they may inspect only documents in the office of the undertaking (paragraph 46, sub paragraph 2, sentence 2 GWB) and, in the case of refusal to furnish the necessary documents, may ask a judge for permission to search. As such measures would constitute acts of sovereignty, the German antitrust authorities would need the permission of the authorities of the foreign State concerned for such inspection of documents abroad. In administrative fine proceedings, however, third parties might be asked informally to produce or disclose all documents without an inspection in the office of the enterprise being necessary. The mailing to a foreign address of a formal request for disclosure or production of documents located abroad would again constitute an act of sovereignty requiring the permission of the foreign state.

The German antitrust authorities have never tried to inspect documents in the office of a foreign enterprise or to ask a foreign enterprise to produce or disclose documents located abroad. However, there have been two cases in which the BKartA sought to ask German enterprises to furnish information relating to foreign subsidiaries or associates of German enterprises abroad as to the market position and trading practices of the parent company of a German subsidiary. It appears, however, that the German cartel authorities have not been successful in enforcing orders to disclose such information. The foreign companies appear to have refused to comply with such requests.

Two examples may serve to illustrate these points:

i) In one case dealing with the maintenance of the retail price of records the BKartA instituted proceedings against a German enterprise alleging that the prices charged by the enterprise were too high and therefore constituted an abuse of the resale price maintenance provisions. In the course of the proceedings the BKartA asked the German enterprise to submit information about the selling prices of its subsidiaries in France, the Netherlands and Great Britain and about retail prices charged. The request was not answered. After a further request the enterprise refused again to provide the information requested. The BKartA then issued a formal request for information pursuant to paragraph 46 GWB. The enterprise appealed against this formal decision, arguing, inter alia, that the decision violated paragraph 98 sub paragraph 2 GWB, as the BKartA was not authorised to ask for information dealing with markets outside Germany. The Kammergericht in its decision pointed out that paragraph 98 sub paragraph 2 GWB was not violated as the request for information contained questions dealing with possible effects within Germany.

– Decision of June 18, 1971, WuW/E OLG 1169 – *Importschallplatten* –.

(ii) The second case concerned a multinational oil company, BP. In the course of its proceedings against the multinational oil concerns during the first oil crisis, the BKartA by a preliminary decision based on paragraph 56 GWB had prohibited certain alleged abuses of a dominant market position consisting of charging prices which it considered too high. The BKartA ordered the immediate enforcement of its decision. The German subsidiary of B.P. appealed against this order. The Kammergericht annulled this decision on the ground that BKartA had proved neither the abuse nor the necessity for the immediate enforcement of its decision. In the reasons for its decision the Kammergericht mentioned that the BKartA had the power to order the German subsidiary of B.P. to supply all the necessary information about the prices charged by its parent company for oil. The court pointed out that such information could also be requested from foreign enterprises through the intermediary of the German subsidiary.

– Decision of May 14, 1974, WuW/E OLG 1467, 169 – *BP* –.

### 4.2.3 Search and investigation of persons or companies abroad

According to German understanding of international law, no searches, investigations or hearings of defendants or witnesses, which constitute acts of sovereignty, are possible without the permission of the foreign State where it is intended to carry them out. The German antitrust authorities have never sought to initiate such proceedings abroad and/or to ask the relevant foreign State for its permission. Although such steps where carried out voluntarily and without any element of compulsion are allowed it appears that the German antitrust authorities have never tried to instigate such voluntary investigations or hearings which, according to the principle of comity in international law as interpreted by German legal theorists, would have to be notified to the authorities of the foreign State.

### 4.2.4 Hearing of defendants or witnesses abroad

See answer to 4.2.3 above.

### 4.2.5 Service of process abroad

Except for such acts of the antitrust authorities as are expressly mentioned by the law as requiring formal service of process, any acts may be communicated to the persons or enterprises concerned by normal letter, telex or any other means of communication available. However, for practical purposes, and in order to prove the receipt of important documents, most other acts are also formally served in antitrust proceedings. In all cases where no formal service of process is required, any communications may be and have been sent abroad directly by the German antitrust authorities.

For both antitrust procedures (administrative and administrative fine proceedings) the German law concerning service of process in administrative matters is applicable (Verwaltungszustellungsgesetz paragraph 57, sub paragraph 1, sentence 1; paragraph 81, paragraph 36, sub paragraph 1, GWB; paragraph 51 OWIG). According to this statute service may be effected by post, either by formal service of process with a special service of process document or by registered letter with or without advice of delivery. Furthermore, if the authority itself effects service of process against a special document of advice, this may be done at any place where the addressee or its legal representative is met. Therefore, theoretically, service of process may be effected upon legal representatives of foreign enterprises when they enter into Germany, i.e. at any German airport. It appears, however, that this has never been attempted.

Because acts of service of process are acts of sovereignty, no direct service of process may be effected abroad without the prior consent of the foreign State. Paragraph 14 VWZG provides that service of process abroad may only be effected through the intermediary of the foreign State by the diplomatic service. As it is not certain in many cases whether the authorities of the foreign State are willing to comply with such a request for service of process and as such a procedure would be protracted, it appears that the German antitrust authorities have never, until recently, sought to make use of these channels.

In a recent case the BKartA for the first time has formally served the statement of objections and the decision imposing an administrative fine to enterprises in several West European countries by the agency of the diplomatic service, either directly through the German diplomatic representatives or through the competent Ministry of Foreign Affairs.

The legal provisions for service of process are formal and exacting. Process is not validly served if the cartel authority merely shows that the addressee of the decision has knowledge of the contents of that decision. (*See* Kammergericht decision of September 19, 1979 in the case of the *Stadtwerke Leverkusen*, WuW/E OLG 2202).

It may be seen that, although there is provision under German antitrust procedure for the execution of various procedural steps abroad, the antitrust authorities have a very high respect for the principles of international law and prefer to rely upon invitations to voluntary compliance with antitrust investigations where the parties are located abroad rather than to risk infringement of international law.

In certain cases German law provides for a 'public' service of process by publication in the Official Gazette.

According to paragraph 15 VwZG (Verwaltungszustellungsgesetz) public service of process is admissible only in cases where service could not be effected through normal channels (such as service upon a competent person within Germany or with the consent of the appropriate authorities in a foreign State).

Where process is served by publication in the Federal Gazette (paragraph 15, sub paragraph 4 VwZG) the enterprise affected must be informed of the public service and of the contents of the documents served by normal letter. According to paragraph 15, sub paragraph 3 VwZG it is presumed that a document which has been published in the Federal Gazette has been served two weeks after such publication.

In the case Bayer France/Firestone France the BKartA published the prohibition in the Federal Gazette only two days prior to the deadline laid down in merger control rules (four months after the filing of a premerger notification). The BKartA had found no means of serving process on Firestone – neither in Germany nor through diplomatic channels in France. The Appellate Court in Berlin ('Kammergericht') ruled that the two weeks waiting period under paragraph 15, sub paragraph 3 VwZG, did not apply in antitrust proceedings. [For further details of this case see 2.2 above.]

### 4.3 EEC

The Commission may initiate proceedings in three ways:

(i) Upon an application for a negative clearance (Reg. 17/62, Art. 2) or an exemption (Reg. 17/62 Art. 4); or

(ii) following a third party complaint (Reg. 17/62, Art. 3(2)); or

(iii) on its own initiative, through individual procedure *ex officio* (Reg.

17/62 Art. 3) or a general inquiry into a sector of the economy (Reg. 17/62, Art. 12).

### 4.3.1 Written requests for information (discovery orders)

Pursuant to Article 11(1) of Regulation 17/62, the Commission may obtain all necessary information from enterprises or associations of enterprises. The powers granted to the Commission are thus not expressly limited to enterprises located within the Community. The requirement under Article 11(2) of Regulation 17/62, to the effect that, before sending a request for information the Commission shall at the same time forward a copy of the request to the competent authority of the Member State in whose territory the seat of the enterprise is located, should not be read to imply a general limitation, or a limitation to the effect that a request for information to an enterprise outside the Community may be sent only to enterprises that belong to a group whose legal seat or principal place of business is within the Community. The requirement is simply a specific application of the general principle established in Article 10(2) of Regulation 17/62, according to which the Commission shall carry out any procedure for the application of Articles 85 and 86 in close and constant liaison with the competent authorities of the Member States, and such authorities shall have the right to express their views upon such a procedure.

Indeed, the Court seems to have recognised implicitly the Commission's power to send a request for information to enterprises located outside the Community. In its decision in *United Brands (Chiquita)* (Case 27/67, [1978] ECR 207), the Court, reviewing the Commission's finding on excessive prices, stated that '[t]he Commission was at least under a duty to require UBC to produce particulars of all the constituent elements of its production costs' (paragraph 256, at p. 302). While the facts of the case do not emerge clearly from the text of the Court's decision, the Court seems to refer to information which was held by UBC outside the Community, since it would have included production costs in Central America and transfer prices. (*See* pp. 244-245). It may be noted, however, that since UBC's subsidiary within the Community was also involved in the proceedings, it is arguable that the Court only referred to the Commission's power to request a company within the Community to supply the Commission with information located outside the Community (*see* Point 4.3.2 below).

Since no EEC measure would limit the Commission's power in this regard, it would seem that any limitation on the Commission's right to send a request for information to enterprises outside the Community would have to be found in the rules of international law rather than in the EEC rules.

The Commission's power to send an informal request for information to enterprises outside the Community should not create a problem under international law. The enterprises are not obliged to respond, and the Commission's request therefore could not be seen as an attempted act of coercion.

Nevertheless, it should be noted, as mentioned in Point 4.3.1 above, that even an informal request for information pursuant to Article 11(3) of Regulation 17, has two precise legal effects which might raise questions under international law. First, if the enterprises outside the Community respond, but supply incorrect information, they are subject to fines. Second, a request for information by a formal decision of the Commission, pursuant to Article 11(5) of Regulation 17, must be preceded by the sending of an informal request for information. Thus the informal request for information is a necessary step in the formal procedure and could be considered a part of it. It appears that the Commission has developed a practice of sending completely informal requests for information, i.e. those which do not contain any reference to Article 11(3) of Regulation 17, and which therefore, would not seem to have the effects mentioned above.

In fact, it is normal practice for the Commission to send an informal request for information to enterprises outside the Community, without going through the authorities of the countries where the enterprises are located and seemingly without informing those authorities of its request. Generally, companies located outside the Community do answer the Commission's informal request for information, although there probably have been cases in which no answer was furnished. It seems for example, that in the *Zoja/Commercial Solvents case* (O.J. No. L 299/51, December 3, 1972) CSS did not answer an informal request for information.

It is more difficult to determine whether international law would limit the power of the Commission to send a formal request for information to enterprises outside the Community. Although the formal request for information would, according to Regulation 17/62, empower the Commission to impose fines or periodic penalty payments in the case of non-compliance or upon finding that the information is incomplete or misleading, the sending of the formal request for information would not seem in itself to constitute an act of coercion which is exercised outside the territory of the Community in such a way as to be incompatible with international law. Indeed, to the extent that the Commission has substantive jurisdiction on the basis of the effects doctrine, (a basis not yet explicitly recognised by the Court), it would seem reasonable that the Commission should have the right to send formal requests for information to enterprises outside the Community.

However, in light of the possible imposition of fines in the case of non-compliance, and quite apart from the question of service of process, (*see* point 5 below), it would seem appropriate for the Commission to inform the authorities and, in particular, the office of foreign affairs of the country where the enterprise is located.

In practice, the Commission seems not to have sent a formal request for information to an enterprise outside the Community.

International law would seem to limit the Commission's power to request information from any enterprise outside the Community if furnishing the information would amount to a violation of the law of the country where the enterprise is located. The Commission does not seem to accept this point of view, as is instanced by the decision in the *CSV* case (O.J. No. L92/27, July 16, 1976).

Finally, non-compliance by an enterprise located outside the Community with the Commission's informal or formal request for information might affect the position of the enterprise in the proceedings before the Commission or, more likely, in proceedings before the Court. With respect to the proceedings before the Commission, should the enterprise choose to furnish the information requested, it would probably be free to do so before the end of the proceedings, for instance, after having received the statement of objections or at the oral hearings. Should the enterprise seek review before the Court of a decision taken by the Commission, it is likely that non-compliance with the Commission's request for information might place a heavier burden of proof on the enterprise. The Commission's decision would be based on facts obtained from sources other than the enterprise concerned and, although there seem to be no cases in point, it is likely that the Court would impose strict standards of proof on the enterprise. It would seem inappropriate for the Court to refuse to consider facts presented by the applicant on the grounds that these facts had not been revealed in response to the Commission's request for information. It is interesting to note that, in the field of breach by the Commission of due process, the Court held in *Hoffmann-la Roche* ('Vitamins' Case 85/76, 1979, ECR 461) that procedural irregularities committed by the Commission could be remedied in the course of the appeal. *A fortiori*, it seems reasonable to conclude that the applicant should be free to choose at which level of the procedure to disclose facts relevant to its defence.

### 4.3.2 Production and disclosure of documents located abroad

The procedural provision here relevant is Article 11 of Regulation 17/62, dealt with under point 4.3.1, above.

(i) It seems clear that the Commission has the power to require information which is located outside the Community but which is under the control of an enterprise located within the Community, for instance, if the information is with a subsidiary outside the Community of a group whose headquarters are within the Community.

(ii) If the information is outside the Community, but the group which controls the information is present within the Community, e.g. through a subsidiary, the Commission should also have the power to obtain the information. On the basis of the economic unit theory, the group is held to be present within the Community and therefore the situation should not be different from that under (i) above.

As mentioned in point 4.3.1 above, the Court, in *United Brands (Chiquita)*, seems to imply that the Commission has the power to request information located outside the Community which is under the control of a non-EEC group, at least when the group has a subsidiary within the Community. Whether the request for information should be addressed to the subsidiary within the Community or to the parent company outside the Community does not seem to be important. In any event, if the Commission issues a formal request for information which is not complied with, the enforcement of fines or periodic penalties would be made against the assets of the subsidiary within the Community.

(iii) When the information is under the control of a group which does not have an establishment within the Community the issue is whether the Commission has the power to send requests for information (*see* point 4.3.1 above).

### 4.3.3 Search and investigation of persons or companies abroad

Pursuant to Article 14(1) of Regulation 17/62, the Commission may undertake all necessary investigations in carrying out the duties assigned to it by Article 89 and by provisions adopted under Article 87 of the Treaty. The powers granted to the Commission are thus not expressly limited to investigations carried out within the Community.

However, the exercise of the Commission's power of investigation outside the Community would seem to constitute a violation of international law, unless exercised in the framework of a treaty or of an agreement between the Community and the country where the investigation is conducted. An investigation of the premises of an enterprise located outside the Community would necessarily appear to constitute an act of coercion exercised in the territory of a sovereign State in violation of international law. It would not be relevant whether the enterprise located outside the Community whose premises were to be investigated belonged to a group whose headquarters were within the Community. While the Commission could obtain the information located abroad through a request addressed to the companies of the group established within the Community (*see* point 4.3.1 above), conducting the investigation abroad would constitute a violation of the sovereignty of the country in which the office investigated was located.

The Community is not party to any treaty or agreement which would allow the Commission to conduct such investigations outside the territory of the Common Market.

### 4.3.4 Hearing of defendants or witnesses abroad

Article 19 of Regulation 17/62 and Regulation 99/63 laying down implementing provisions concerning hearings do not specify where such hearings will take place. The organisation of the hearings is left to the discretion of the Commission on the basis of the provisions of Regulation 99/63. Article 8(1) provides that the Commission shall summon the persons to be heard to attend on such date as it shall appoint. Furthermore, pursuant to Article 8(2), Member States may appoint an official to take part in the hearing. The hearing shall be conducted by the persons appointed by the Commission for that purpose (Article 9(1)). Thus, all hearings have been conducted by Commission officials.

On the basis of these provisions and the fact that the hearings are an intrinsic part of the administrative procedure, the possibility of holding hearings outside the Community seems to be excluded.

### 4.3.5 Service of process abroad

The second paragraph of Article 191 of the Treaty of Rome provides that 'decisions shall be notified to those to whom they are addressed and shall take effect upon such notification.' The Court considers that, to the extent that the addressee of the decision has been put in a position to take cognizance of it, the decision is duly notified.

In a case involving the Treaty of Paris (Case 8/56, *Accierie Laminatoi Magliano Alpi* (ALMA) *contre Haute Autorité de la Communauté Européenne du Charbon et de l'Acier*, [1957] Rec. 179, 190) the Court held that where notification is required during the course of administrative proceedings, it is sufficient that the document of which notification is made should duly reach the inner structure of the addressee ('regulièrement entrée dans la sphère interne du destinataire').

In the Dyestuffs cases (Cases 48/69, 52/69 and 53/69; *ICI, Geigy, Sandoz*, [1972], ECR 619, 787 and 845), the Commission had notified its decision to the subsidiaries located within the Community. The applicants argued that their subsidiaries had not been given any authority by the parent companies to accept the notification and that, under the applicable national law, the subsidiaries were under no duty to bring the documents in question to the attention of the parent companies. The Court held that irregularities in the procedure for notification of a decision do not invalidate the decision, but may in certain circumstances prevent the period within which an application to the Court must be lodged from starting to run. Pursuant to the third paragraph of Article 173 of the Treaty, the period for instituting proceedings for the annulment of individual measures of the Commission starts to run from the date of notification of the decision to the applicant or, in the absence thereof, from the date on which it comes to the knowledge of the latter. The Court thus stated that, since it was established that the applicant had full knowledge of the text of the decision and had exercised its right to institute proceedings within the prescribed period, the question of possible irregularities concerning the notification ceased to be relevant.

In Continental Can (Case 6/72 *Europemballage and Continental Can v.*

*Commission* [1973] ECR 215, 241, paragraphs 9-10), the applicant had argued that the decision should have been notified through diplomatic channels, while the applicant had only received one or two letters from the Commission by mail. The Court stated that '[A] decision is properly notified within the meaning of the Treaty, if it reaches the addressee and puts the latter in a position to take cognizance of it. This was so in the present case, because the contested decision actually reached Continental and the latter cannot make use of its own refusal to take cognizance of the decision in order to render this communication ineffective.'

Pursuant to Article 2(1) of Regulation 99/63 the Commission shall inform enterprises or associations of enterprises *in writing* of the objections raised against them. The communication shall be addressed to each of them or to a joint agent appointed by them. Pursuant to Article 2(2), the Commission may inform the parties by giving notice in the Official Journal of the European Communities if this appears appropriate, given the circumstances of the case, in particular, where notice is to be given to a number of undertakings but no joint agent has been appointed. A fine or a periodic penalty payment may be imposed on an enterprise or association of enterprises only if the objections were notified in the manner provided for in paragraph (1) *i.e.* in writing (Article 2(3)). There is no special provision for service of the statement of objections to an enterprise outside the Community.

With respect to the statement of objections, the Court followed the same approach it took with respect to decisions, considering that a statement of objections served in accordance with the EEC rules to a party located in a third country cannot invalidate the subsequent administrative procedure, once it is established that by enabling the addressee to take cognizance of the objections held against him it has achieved its purpose.

The Court took this approach in the *Dyestuffs* cases (Case 52/69 and 53/69 *Geigy, Sandoz* [1972] ECR pp. 823-824 and 845). The applicants complained that the Commission served the notice of objection in a manner inconsistent with Swiss law, the place where the notice was to be served, because the Swiss Confederation does not recognise the validity of service by post of a foreign measure of this kind on its territory. The applicants thus argued that the notice was null and void and that this irregularity gave rise to an infringement of the applicant's right to be heard. The Court held that the purpose of the notice of objections provided for in Article 2(1) of Regulation 99/63 is to enable those concerned to put forward their arguments in the context of proceedings initiated against them. The Court continued:

> 'Since there is no convention on the matter between the Community and the Swiss Confederation, the question of how this notice is to be served on interested parties established outside the territory of the Community depends on international practice and must be resolved with mutual regard to the spheres of jurisdiction both of the Community and of the third State concerned.

It appears from the file that the authorities of the third State in question do not for the present envisage any practical possibility of service, considered by them to be valid under internal law, on the territory of that State.

Therefore, international law cannot be invoked in order to deny the Community the power to take the necessary steps to ensure the effectiveness of measures taken with a view to curtailing conduct adversely affecting competition which has arisen in the Common Market, even if the registered office of the undertaking responsible for such conduct is situated in a third country.

Furthermore, the main purpose of the notice in question is to ensure that those concerned may exercise the rights which they enjoy under the Treaty and Community legislation.

Therefore, a notice served in accordance with Community rules cannot be considered to invalidate the subsequent administrative procedure if it must be served in a third country, once it is established that by enabling the addressee to take cognizance of the objections held against him it has achieved its purpose.'

One may speculate about what would happen in a case in which companies located in a country which had no convention with the Community on the service of process would have returned unanswered the letter received containing the Commission's objections. There would seem to be three options for the Commission. First, since by hypothesis the letter had reached the enterprise, the Commission could consider on the basis of the Court rulings in *ALMA*, in the *Dyestuffs* and *Continental Can* cases that 'by enabling the addressee to take cognizance of the objections held against him it has achieved its purpose', and that the addressee's refusal to take the cognizance of the objections does not affect the validity of the notification.

Second, if one of the EEC Member States did have a convention with the third country in question providing for specific procedures for the service of process, the Commission could require the authorities of the Member State to make the notification of the Commission's objections in the form provided for in the convention, on the basis of the general principle of co-operation between the Commission and the authorities of the Member States implicit in Regulation 17/62 (*see*, in particular, Article 14 (b)). Finally, the Commission could publish the statement of objections in the Official Journal of the European Communities, pursuant to Article 2(2) of Regulation 99/63. In this case, pursuant to Article 2(3) of Regulation 99/63, the enterprise notified of the Commission's objections through the publication in the Official Journal would not seem to be subject to the imposition of fines.

## 4.4 FRANCE

### 4.4.1 Written requests for information (discovery orders)

The Ordonnance 45/1484 of 30 June 1945 and the Loi of 19 July 1977, do not provide for any possibility of written requests for information being sent outside national boundaries by the Commission de la Concurrence.

In cases of price fixing sanctioned under Art. 419 of the French Criminal Code, and in such cases as are transferred to the Public Prosecutor's Office for action pursuant to the Ordonnance of 30 June 1945, it appears possible, under general criminal procedural rules, for the investigating magistrate in charge of the case to send out international letters rogatory. By these, foreign judicial authorities are requested to carry out investigations complementary to those made on French territory. It is up to the authorities to whom the letters rogatory are directed to determine whether, under the laws of their country, such letters rogatory are admissible or not.

Apart from specific Treaty provisions, all letters rogatory which aim at accomplishing acts of discovery known under French law are considered permissible under French law: orders for the taking of depositions, the hearing of witnesses, search and seizure etc. to the extent that an international treaty has been signed and that the act requested is known by the laws of the State whose assistance has been requested.

In the case of a claim for damages for infringement of antitrust law lodged before the Commercial Court such a claim, although based upon a criminal provision, might be considered to be of a commercial nature. Then, it would seem that the Convention on the taking of Evidence Abroad in civil or commercial matters done at the Hague on March 18 1970, would be applicable (*see* 11.1.2 below).

### 4.4.2 Production and disclosure of documents located abroad

There is no provision for the production and disclosure of documents located abroad, other than by way of letters rogatory (*see* 4.4.1).

### 4.4.3 Search and investigation of persons or companies abroad

Apart from international discovery orders in criminal proceedings (described under 4.4.1 above) there is no provision for such search and investigation. No such international discovery order has been sent out.

### 4.4.4 Hearing of defendants or witnesses abroad

Defendants or witnesses may only be heard outside national territory in antitrust proceedings in the case of international letters rogatory (*see* 4.4.1 above).

### 4.4.5 Service of process abroad

There is no specific provision under French law for service of process outside national boundaries with respect to letters or decisions in administrative antitrust proceedings.

However, the French government has signed International Conventions for service of administrative documents abroad (e.g. with some African countries).

In the case of criminal proceedings, the general provisions of the Code of Criminal Procedure apply.

Service of process is made on the basis of International Conventions, by the French judicial authorities through diplomatic channels in the following stages:

- service of the claim;
- service of the citation to appear before the Court;
- service of the extradition request.

## 4.5 U.K.

The material provisions of the U.K. antitrust law have only very limited potential for extraterritorial application. The statutes are based on the premise that U.K. courts have not yet generally assumed jurisdiction over persons or enterprises whose business activities take place outside the U.K.; legislation provides no rules concerning extraterritorial procedure.

### 4.5.1 Written requests for information (discovery orders)

Where, in the most exceptional circumstances, it were considered desirable to obtain information from persons outside the U.K., enquiries might be made of such persons on a purely voluntary basis, with due regard to international comity.

### 4.5.2 Production and disclosure of documents located abroad

Documents located abroad may not be obtained for use by the DGFT. Only where the person requested to produce the documents is within the territorial jurisdiction and that person has control over the documents located abroad, may production and disclosure be ordered by a court: Order 24, Rule 3(i) of RSC.

In the recent decision of the Court of Appeal in the case *Lonhro Ltd. and Another v. Shell Petroleum Co. Limited and Another* it was held that in the case of multinational companies located abroad, it is a question of fact whether a parent company has in its 'power' documents in the possession of its overseas subsidiaries. Relevant factors in determining whether such power exists will be the degree of managerial autonomy of the subsidiaries, whether local laws forbid the production of the documents and the commercial interests of the subsidiary concerned.

### 4.5.3 Search and investigation of persons or companies abroad

There is no provision for such searches to be conducted abroad under U.K. law.

### 4.5.4 Hearing of defendants or witnesses abroad

Depositions may be conducted, but only on a voluntary basis.

### 4.5.5 Service of process abroad

Order 11 of the RSC (1965) is the relevant provision here. The order provides for service of a writ out of the jurisdiction in a certain limited number of cases with the leave of the court, (Order 11, rule I). Certain of the categories of cases listed might apply to antitrust actions (e.g. rule I, (e), (f), (i)) but in practice it is the policy of the DGFT not to seek service abroad, and the possibility would therefore only arise in civil actions.

None of the situations encompassed by the provisions of Order 11 are analogous to private antitrust actions under U.S. law. In the case of *George Munroe Limited v. American Cyanamid* the court recognised that leave for service out of the jurisdiction should only be granted after careful consideration as the area is so contentious.

## 4.6 SWITZERLAND

In cases of civil law actions brought by private parties to enforce rights and remedies against restraints of trade, the cantonal code of civil procedure of the cantonal court with jurisdiction applies. The general rules of international civil procedure apply in the absence of bilateral or multilateral treaties.

The Federal Court has made it clear that the attitude of Swiss law towards extraterritorial application of rules which ultimately serve the protection of the Swiss economic order would be reserved.

There is no enforcement power of the Cartels Commission beyond that of the compulsory taking of evidence in proceedings opened in the course of a special enquiry. The procedural rules governing this power are found in the Federal Code of Civil Procedure. Art. 39 of the Code states that evidence has to be taken by way of judicial assistance i.e. by letters of request addressed to the competent authority of the State concerned. Swiss courts rely on the principle of international comity and will expect compliance with a request on that basis. There is no instance of such letters of request having been issued in administrative matters. This includes antitrust matters in respect of which Switzerland will not grant judicial assistance to foreign states as a matter of policy and will therefore not expect compliance with a request addressed to a foreign state as a matter of comity.

## 4.7 ITALY

Italy has no antitrust legislation other than EEC rules.

## 4.8 AUSTRALIA

### 4.8.1 Written requests for information (discovery orders)

Section 155 of the Trade Practices Act 1974 enables the Trade Practices Commission (the body administering the Act) to seek particulars, obtain information and require production of documents in relation to any matter that it alleges may constitute a contravention of the Act. Section 156 enables the person authorised by the Commission to inspect such documents produced in pursuance of a Notice under Section 155 or indeed to make copies of those documents. Failure to comply with a Notice received under Section 155 renders the person liable to a pecuniary penalty.

However, Sections 155 and 156 do not fall within Parts IV and V of the Act and, based on the reasoning set out previously, it may therefore be concluded that extraterritoriality has not been intended. There is certainly no express intention in the Act to extend the operation of these sections outside Australia and so, on the basis that for a section to apply extraterritorially such an intention must be expressed, one concludes that these sections are restricted to Australian operation and that therefore they could not compel an overseas corporation or person to furnish answers to questions, supply information or produce documents.

### 4.8.2 Production and disclosure of documents located abroad

The Trade Practices Act 1974 is an Act containing substantive rather than procedural law. The Federal Court Rules of Procedure would apply to actions brought in that court under the Act. The rule applicable here would be Order 15, Rule 1 which states:

> '1. After a directions hearing pursuant to Order 10 and within any period limited by the Court for this purpose, any party may, unless the Court otherwise orders, by notice of discovery filed and served on any other party, require any other party to give discovery of documents.'

Therefore, if a corporation is outside the jurisdiction of the Court and does not consent to its jurisdiction, and there is no one within the jurisdiction against whom the Court may enforce its orders, the rules are also rendered unenforceable.

### 4.8.3 Search and investigation of persons or companies abroad

There is no power in the Trade Practices Commission under the Act to search and investigate persons or companies outside the jurisdiction.

### 4.8.4 Hearing of defendants or witnesses abroad

Order 24 Rule 1 of the Federal Court Rules states:

> 'The Court may, for the purpose of proceedings in the Court, make orders;
>
> (a) for the examination of any person on oath before a Judge or be-before such other person as the Court may appoint as examiner at any place whether in or out of Australia; or
>
> (b) for the sending of a letter of request to the judicial authorities of another country to take or cause to be taken, the evidence of any person.'

A party can be subpoenaed either to attend or to produce documents. Failure to comply with the subpoena can mean that the Federal Court can then order that the person attend the examination or produce a document. There is no distinction in the rules as to whether the person the subject of such an order is a witness or a defendant. Indeed, if a defendant does not submit to the jurisdiction of the Court, then it would be feasible that, if this evidence was necessary for the plaintiff's case to succeed, (a highly improbable proposition) the Court could order the evidence to be taken by deposition.

### 4.8.5 Service of process abroad

Order 8 Rule 1(b) of the Federal Court Rules provides that:

> '1(b) Where the proceeding is founded on a breach of an Act, where the breach is committed in the Commonwealth ... originating process may be served outside the Commonwealth.'

Once the originating process has been served, the Court procedure then adopts the normal course, except that if the corporation appears, service can be effected on its solicitor.

# 5. Channels used in procedural matters

## 5.0 INTRODUCTION

In view of the existence of provisions for taking procedural steps outside the jurisdiction in many legal systems, it is appropriate to consider next which channels are normally used for such procedures by those States which do exercise extraterritorial jurisdiction in antitrust matters, i.e., how such national provisions are put into practice.

Because of the doctrine of State sovereignty, the enforcement of national antitrust law outside national boundaries must depend largely upon the good nature of the State within whose territory it is required to proceed. If process is to be served by U.S. antitrust authorities upon a French or Swiss company, the successful conclusion of the necessary procedure will be heavily dependent upon the goodwill of the French or Swiss authorities. Thus, for example, in the *Dyestuffs* cases before the European Court of Justice, the Commission revealed that both the British Ambassador and the Swiss Ambassador, refused to forward notification of the Decision to a subsidiary established within the EEC.

## 5.1 WRITTEN REQUESTS FOR INFORMATION (DISCOVERY ORDERS)

### *USA*

The procedure in the U.S. is for informal requests for information to be addressed to the private party concerned, subsequent to the notification of the appropriate authority of the requested State. Where formal requests are involved, such demands are subject to the requirement of service (*see* 5.5 below).

### *Germany*

Where a formal decision containing a request for information is to be sent abroad, formal service of process is required (*see* 5.5 below) and hence the prior consent and assistance of the authorities of the foreign state.

In a number of cases, informal requests for information have been addressed to foreign addressees by way of normal mail. There is no element of compulsion involved in such requests.

### *EEC*

In the case of a formal request for information sent under Reg. 17/62 Art. 2(5), which may lead to the imposition of fines for non-compliance, it would seem appropriate for the authorities of the country where the enterprise is located to be informed; with regard to Member States, this is provided for by Art. 10 of Reg. 17/62. It is normal practice for the Commission to send an informal request for information to enterprises outside the Community without going through the authorities of the country where the addressee is located, and, seemingly, without informing these authorities of its request. (For the EFTA countries and Israel, see 11. below).

*France*

In the case of administrative proceedings there is no provision, but the prior consent and assistance of the authorities of the foreign State should be requested.

In the case of criminal proceedings, requests for information may only be issued in the form of letters rogatory addressed to the competent authority of the requested States.

Discovery orders must normally follow diplomatic channels. Yet, in the case of emergency, the Loi of 10 March 1977, provides 'that discovery orders can be the subject of direct communications between the judicial authorities of both States.'

*U.K.*

Where, in exceptional circumstances, it was considered necessary to obtain information from persons outside the U.K., inquiries might be made of these persons on a purely voluntary basis with a proper regard for international comity.

*Switzerland*

Art. 39 of the Federal Code of Civil Procedure states that evidence has to be taken by way of letters of request (letters rogatory) addressed to the competent authority of the requested State.

*Australia*

As yet, there has been no case in which the authorities have been unable to find someone within the jurisdiction upon whom the section 155 Notice could be served. The overseas operation of a section 155 Notice has not, therefore, been considered (*see* 4.8 above).

## 5.2 PRODUCTION AND DISCLOSURE OF DOCUMENTS

*USA*

The procedure for 'civil investigative demands' (outlined under 5.1 above) applies also to documentary material pertinent to antitrust investigations.

United States federal courts take the position that they have the authority to require directly the production of documents located abroad where the court has *in personam* jurisdiction over the person or entity in possession or control of the material.

*Germany*

The cartel authority may, in administrative proceedings, inspect documents only in the office of the undertaking and, in case of a refusal to submit the necessary documents, may ask a judge to give permission to search. Since such steps are seen as acts of sovereignty, the antitrust authority would need the permission of the authorities of the foreign State for such investigation of documents abroad.

In administrative fine proceedings, the posting of a request for the disclosure of production of documents located abroad (in the hands of third parties) to foreign addressees would again constitute an act of sovereignty, which would need the permission of the foreign State.

*EEC*

Where the documents are under the control of a group which does not also have an establishment within the Community, the issue is whether the Commission has power to send requests for information (*see* point 5.1 above).

*France*

No provision in administrative proceedings. In criminal proceedings by way of letters rogatory.

*U.K.*

No provision.

*Switzerland*

The procedure in administrative proceedings would be by way of letters rogatory (*see* 5.1 above).

*Australia*

No provision.

## 5.3 SEARCH AND INVESTIGATION OF PERSONS OR COMPANIES

*USA*

The antitrust authorities do investigate, on a voluntary basis only, where both the persons concerned and the foreign government concerned have no objection. It is their policy to advise the foreign government concerned before conducting the interview. The U.S. Government follows the recommendations of the OECD relating to inter-governmental notification in these situations (*see* 11.1.3 below).

*Germany*

Any searches or investigations which constitute acts of sovereignty are not possible without the permission of the foreign State where it is intended to carry them out. There has never been an attempt to initiate such a procedure.

If the element of compulsion is seen as essential in defining an act of public authority (act of sovereignty), then such measures carried out voluntarily would be allowed. The principle of international comity would in any event require notification of the authorities of the foreign State. Such voluntary proceedings have also never been attempted.

*EEC*

The exercise of the Commission's power of investigation outside the Community would appear to constitute a violation of international law, unless exercised in the framework of the agreement between the Community and the country where the investigation is conducted. It would necessarily constitute an act of sovereignty exercised in the territory of a foreign State. The Commission seems not to have attempted any such investigation.

*France*

No provision, beyond 5.1 above: letters rogatory.

*U.K.*

No provision.

*Switzerland*

No provision, beyond application for judicial assistance by way of letters rogatory, in administrative proceedings.

*Australia*

No provision.

## 5.4 HEARING OF DEFENDANTS OR WITNESSES

*USA*

A defendant or witness may agree to a deposition being conducted outside the United States in connection with an antitrust proceeding. Both parties' counsel are entitled to be present to question the deponent. The statement of a defendant or witness outside the country can sometimes be presented by sworn affidavit.

There appear to be no further formalities of procedure either required or observed.

*Germany*

The hearing of defendants or witnesses is seen as an act of sovereignty, and as such not possible without the permission of the foreign state where it is intended to be conducted.

It has never been attempted to carry out such measures voluntarily and without any element of compulsion, although, so conducted, they may not constitute acts of sovereignty. In any event, German understanding of the international law principle of comity would require even such voluntary measures to be notified to the authorities of the foreign State concerned.

*EEC*

The possibility of holding hearings outside the Community seems to be excluded.

*France*

The only procedure available, and that only in criminal proceedings, is letters rogatory issued by the investigating magistrate.

*U.K.*

Witnesses or defendants might, exceptionally, be heard outside the jurisdiction, but only on a voluntary basis, and with due regard to international comity. This would require notification to and the consent of the appropriate authority of the State concerned.

*Switzerland*

No provision other than Art. 39 Federal Code of Civil Procedure which provides for the issue of letters rogatory.

*Australia*

Where it is sought to obtain evidence from a witness located abroad, the party requesting such evidence must apply to the Court. If the Court is satisfied that it is a proper request in the interest of justice to the parties, it will then send a letter of request for evidence to be taken, together with a list of interrogatories, to the appropriate Tribunal in the foreign country concerned. Neither the Attorney General nor the Foreign Affairs Department need be notified.

## 5.5 SERVICE OF PROCESS

*USA*

Rule 4(d) (3) of the Federal Rules of Civil Procedure provides for service upon a domestic or foreign corporation, 'by delivering a copy of the summons and of the complaint to an officer, a managing or general agent, or to any other agent authorised by appointment or by law to receive service of process and, if the agent is one authorised by statute to receive service and the statute so requires, by also mailing a copy to the defendant.'

Rule 4(i) gives 'Alternative Provisions for Service in a Foreign Country':

> (1) Manner. When the federal or state law referred to in subdivision (e) of this rule authorises service upon a party not an inhabitant of or found within the state in which the district court is held, and service is to be effected upon the party in a foreign country, it is also sufficient if service of the summons and complaint is made: (A) in the manner prescribed by the law of the foreign country for service in that country in an action in any of its courts of general jurisdiction; or (B) as directed by the foreign authority in response to a letter rogatory, when service in either case is reasonably calculated to give actual notice; or (C) upon an individual, by delivery to him personally, and upon a corporation or partnership or association, by delivery to an officer, a managing or general agent; or (D) by any form of mail, requiring a signed receipt, to be addressed and dispatched by the clerk of the court to the party to be served; or (E) as directed by order of the court. Service under (C) or (E) above may be made by any person who is not a party and is not less than 18 years of age or who is designated by order of the district court or by the foreign court. On request, the

clerk shall deliver the summons to the plaintiff for transmission to the person or the foreign court or officer who will make the service.

(2) Return. Proof of service may be made as prescribed by subdivision (g) of this rule, or by the law of the foreign country, or by order of the court. When service is made pursuant to subparagraph (1) (D) of this subdivision, proof of service shall include a receipt signed by the addressee or other evidence of delivery to the addressee satisfactory to the court.

As amended Jan. 21, 1963, eff. July 1, 1963; Feb. 28, 1966, eff. July 1, 1966.

There appears on the face of Rule 4(i) to be no provision for the notification of service to the foreign government or other authority concerned.

*Germany*

For both administrative and administrative fine procedures, the applicable law regarding service is the Verwaltungszustellungsgesetz (VwZG). According to this law, service may be effected by post, either by a formal service of process with a special service of process document, or by registered letter, with or without advice of delivery. Furthermore, if the authority itself carries out the service of process against a special document of advice, this may be done at any place where the addressee or its legal representative is found. Therefore, theoretically, service of process may be effected to legal representatives of foreign enterprises when they enter Germany, e.g. at any German airport. This has, however, never been attempted in practice.

Because acts of service are acts of sovereignty, no direct service of process may be effected abroad without the prior consent of the foreign State. Paragraph 14 VwZG provides that any service of process abroad may only be effected through the intermediary of the foreign State via the diplomatic service. This procedure has recently been used for the first time (*see* 4.2.5 above).

*EEC*

A decision is properly served under EEC law when it reaches the addressee and puts the latter in a position to take cognizance of it. No special form is required for service of process outside the Community. Art. 191 (2) of the EEC Treaty provides that ‘decisions shall be notified to those to whom they are addressed and shall take effect upon such notification.’ In the *ALMA Case* the European Court of Justice held that it is sufficient that the document by which notification is made should duly reach the inner structure of the addressee. In the *Dyestuffs* decision, it was held that irregularities in the procedure for notification do not invalidate the decision, but may in certain circumstances prevent the period in which an appeal to the Court must be lodged from starting to run.

In *Continental Can v. Commission*, the applicant argued that the decision should have been notified through diplomatic channels, while the applicant had only received one or two letters from the Commission by mail. The Court refused to take this point.

Where a notice of objection is concerned, the Court has taken the same approach (*Dyestuffs, Geigy, Sandoz*). In the *Geigy* and *Sandoz* cases the Court said:

> 'It appears from the file that the authorities of the third state in question (Switzerland) do not ... envisage any practical possibility of service, considered by them to be valid under internal law, on the territory of that State. Therefore, international law cannot be invoked in order to deny the Community the power to take the necessary steps to ensure the effectiveness of measures taken with a view to curtailing conduct adversely affecting competition which has arisen in the Common Market, even if the registered office of the undertaking responsible for such conduct is situated in a third country.'

*France*

In administrative proceedings, there is no provision for service of process outside France.

In criminal proceedings, service of process is made according to International Treaties (*see* 4.4.5 above).

*U.K.*

On those rare occasions where it might be required that service of process be made outside the jurisdiction, the applicable procedural rules may be found in Order 11, Rules 3, 5-8. The writ itself is served in other parts of the British Isles (i.e. outside England and Wales), but in other States notice of the writ is served. In the absence of an International Convention, service must be effected by private arrangement and may either be in accordance with English or with local law. The leave of the Court is required for service out of the jurisdiction. Notice may be served, generally, either through the judicial authorities of the country (where a Civil Procedure Convention subsists, other than the Hague Convention), or through the government of that country, except where service through such an authority is contrary to the law of that country. Order 11 Rule 6.

*Switzerland*

In administrative matters there is no provision.

*Australia*

The Federal Court Rules, in Order 8 Rule 1(b) provide that originating process may be served outside the Commonwealth. Service need not be made upon the defendant personally provided that it is made in accordance with the law of the country in which service is effected. Where parties to an International Convention are concerned, it is necessary to prepare the document for service and forward it to the registry for sealing. The Registrar will then send that document to the Attorney General for transmission to the foreign country where service is to be effected. (Order 8 Rule 10). Where a certificate purporting to be a certificate of a judicial authority or other responsible person in the country concerned, or a British or Australian consular authority, as to service or attempted service is filed, that certificate shall be evidence of the matters stated in it (Order 8 Rule 11).

Should service not take place in Convention countries service must be in accordance with the laws of the country concerned.

# 6. National provisions for remedies in the event of a failure to comply with requests for information

## 6.0 INTRODUCTION

This problem has two aspects which must be clearly distinguished.

First, there must be considered what remedies might be available to a person requesting information against the defendant or witness located abroad. Where the medium of letters rogatory is used, then the judicial authorities of the State whose assistance is thereby requested may also have remedies at their disposal.

Secondly, there is the issue of what effect a refusal by a defendant or witness located abroad to supply information might have upon the position of the plaintiff in an action brought within the jurisdiction from which the request for information originated.

The question of enforcement of any remedies must also be considered, although this should not give rise to any major difficulties as, in each case outlined above, there is no question of extraterritorial jurisdiction being asserted. Rather, the authorities involved are acting within the boundaries of their own territory in circumstances where they have assumed jurisdiction to do so.

Various remedies fall for consideration:

### *a) Remedies*

Where information is refused, and the defendant is present in some form within the jurisdiction which is seeking to compel discovery, then the defendant's assets present within that territory may be made the object of fines or seizure in an attempt to enforce supply of the information held abroad.

### *b) Effects*

The refusal to supply information located abroad may have an effect upon the position of the defendant at the trial, in shifting the burden of proof or in raising certain presumptions against him. Similarly, it may affect his position in proceedings or investigations conducted by an administrative authority.

### *c) Letters Rogatory*

Where the assistance of the judicial authorities of another State have been invoked by way of letters rogatory, then those authorities will possess a discretion to use such sanctions for a refusal to supply information as seem to them appropriate. Within common law systems, the power to declare a witness in contempt of court is a particularly potent weapon, for the discretion as to sanctions in that event is very broad. The requesting authority may also have sanctions available in the event of a failure to comply with letters rogatory.

## 6.1 USA

### *a) Remedies*

Where witnesses in foreign countries are concerned, subpoenas may be directed to compel appearance as a witness or production of documents only in the limited circumstances provided by Section 1783 of the Judicial Code, i.e., only where the witness concerned is a citizen of or a resident of the United States. (Rule 45 Fed. R. Civ. P. provides the authority for the issue of such subpoenas, for discovery or trial). 'In a criminal case the person's testimony or document production must be necessary in the interest of justice. In a civil case, in addition to the showing of necessity it must be shown that "it is not possible to obtain his testimony in admissible form without his personal appearance or to obtain the production of the document or other thing in any other manner." ' (E. Kintner & M. Joelson, *An International Antitrust Primer* 50 (1974).

Where there is a failure to comply with such a subpoena, the issuing court may make an order to show cause and direct that the person's property within the U.S. be held as security for a possible fine of not more than $ 100,000 (29 USC § 1784).

Aliens who reside in the U.S. may also be subject to such subpoenas, but non-resident aliens are immune.

The Antitrust Civil Process Act Amendments provide, in the case of civil investigative demands served upon persons in foreign countries, that, 'To the extent that the courts of the United States can assert jurisdiction over such person consistent with due process, the United States District Court for the District of Columbia shall have the same jurisdiction to take any action respecting compliance with this Chapter by any person that such court would have if such person were personally within the jurisdiction of such court.' (15 USC § 1312 (d) (2).) Where jurisdiction exists under this standard, a failure to comply may presumably be treated as contempt of court.

### *b) Effects*

So far as one of the parties to a lawsuit is concerned, failure to comply with a discovery order of a court may result in the imposition of a variety of sanctions provided by Rule 37 of the Federal Rules of Civil Procedure (*see* Appendix 1).

*c) Letters Rogatory*

The United States courts, when assisting the courts of another jurisdiction through the medium of letters rogatory, have a number of remedies available to enforce compliance by a witness, including the power to declare him in contempt of court for a refusal to supply information. No witness may, however, be forced to answer self-incriminating questions, under the Fifth Amendment of the U.S. Constitution.

## 6.2 GERMANY

*a) Remedies*

The German cartel authorities theoretically have the capacity to impose fines upon a foreign undertaking or person for non-compliance with a request for information. The fine may be a sum up to DM 50,000 (paragraph 39, sub paragraph 2 GWB). The decision imposing such a fine would have to be formally served but, after such formal service of process, the decision could theoretically be executed by seizing the property of the foreign undertaking or person within Germany, e.g. the shares of a German subsidiary or affiliate or real estate within Germany. It appears that the BKartA is of the opinion that such an execution would be legal. It has, however, never been attempted in practice (*Scandinavian Paper Case*).

*b) Effects*

If a foreign undertaking is asking for the permission of the German cartel authorities for e.g. a cartel, the non-compliance with a request for information on a voluntary basis may have the effect that the permission is not granted, on the ground that the cartel authorities have not been furnished with the necessary information. Furthermore, in merger cases the time limit within which the BKartA must decide whether a merger has to be prohibited does not run if the information requested according to paragraph 23 sub paragraph 6 GWB is not submitted (paragraph 24 sub paragraph 2 sentence 2 in conjunction with paragraph 24 sub paragraph 2 sentence 2 No. 6 GWB).

*c) Letters Rogatory*

Only in the field of civil or commercial law and to a certain extent in criminal matters the German courts may assist foreign jurisdictions in taking evidence abroad. The Federal Republic of Germany is a party to the Hague Convention on the taking of evidence abroad in civil or commercial matters (see below 11.1.2). In accordance with article 23 of the Convention Germany has declared that it will not execute letters of request issued for the purpose of obtaining pretrial discovery of documents as known in common law countries.

Accordingly, paragraph 14 of the German law implementing the Hague Convention provides that any such letters of request will not be executed. However, paragraph 14 sub paragraph 2 of the said law opens the possibility that insofar as fundamental principles of German procedural law are not affected, such letters of request for pretrial discovery of documents may be executed, if the reasonable interests of the parties involved have been protected by a special regulation which may be issued by the Federal Minister of Justice with the approval of the Bundesrat (representation of the German 'Länder'). However, no such regulation has to date been issued. The competent authorities have declared that they are preparing such a regulation allowing the execution of letters of request for the pretrial discovery of documents to a limited extent and under the control of the German courts in order to avoid German companies being made subject to direct measures especially by the U.S. antitrust authorities in the U.S.

Recently, a U.S. court issued a letter of request to the competent German authorities in a patent violation action, *Corning Glassworks* v. *ITT*. In a counteraction for damages ITT has alleged that Corning participated with other enterprises (including the German company Siemens A.G.) in an antitrust violation. In its letter of request the U.S. court requested both the hearing of witnesses and discovery of documents dealing with the alleged antitrust violation. The competent German authority, in accordance with article 23 of the Convention in conjunction with paragraph 14 sub paragraph 1 of the German law executing the Convention, has ordered that the letter of request shall not be executed insofar as it deals with the pretrial discovery of documents. The letter of request has been transmitted to the competent local court insofar as the hearing of witnesses is concerned.

Both ITT and Siemens A.G. as well as some of the witnesses to be heard appealed against the decision to the Munich court of Appeal which had jurisdiction. The Appeals were dismissed in two decisions of October 31, 1980 and November 27, 1980.

There has been much discussion in Germany of how far the execution of a letter of request might be refused in antitrust matters on the basis of article 12 of the Convention. Article 12 § 1 provides that execution may be refused if the state addressed considers that its sovereignty or security would be prejudiced by the execution. It is argued that the notion of 'sovereignty' covers all aspects of public policy (ordre public). In the case of letters of request dealing with the hearing of witnesses or experts in pretrial discovery procedures of U.S. courts it has been argued that such pretrial discovery procedures violate the principle of German procedural law that no 'searching out of evidence' (Ausforschungsbeweis) is allowed. It appears that the courts have not yet reached any conclusion upon this question. In a similar case involving a letter of request from an Austrian court, the objection of the party involved that the request would violate the above-mentioned principle of procedural law was not taken by the court of appeal concerned. The Munich Court of Appeal, in its decision of Nov. 27 1980 also refused to accept this argument.

Further, it was argued that certain civil or commercial procedures of U.S. law, especially treble damage suits and certain structural reliefs, would offend against German public policy. The Munich Court of Appeal refused to accept this argument.

If the letter of request is not refused for the above-mentioned reasons the competent German authority transmits the request to the competent local court (Amtsgericht). In the case of a request for the hearing of witnesses, article 11 of the Convention may become relevant with regard to certain special privileges of German law whereby a person may refuse to give evidence. Quite apart from the constitutional principle whereby no one may be forced to incriminate himself, paragraph 404 of the German Aktiengesetz may become relevant when dealing with the duty of the members of the board of management or of the supervisory board or of the auditor or assistant auditor of a German Aktiengesellschaft not to disclose confidential information, in particular trade secrets, the violation of which duty may be punished by imprisonment or high fines.

## 6.3 EEC

### *a) Remedies*

The Commission has power to impose fines on enterprises located outside the Community who submit incomplete information in response to an informal request for information, who do not comply with a formal request for information, or who submit incorrect or misleading information. (Reg. 17/62, Art. 15 (1) (b)). The level of the fine may range from 100 to 5,000 U.A. (Units of Account). The Commission may also impose periodic penalty payments in order to compel an enterprise located outside the Community to supply complete and correct information requested by formal decisions. These payments may range from 50 to 1,000 U.A. per day (Reg. 17/62. Art. 16 (1) (c)).

Such decisions are presumably subject to service under Art. 191 (2) EEC. The enforcement of the decisions on companies outside the Community may only be made against assets located within the Community and belonging to that enterprise.

Pursuant to Art. 13 (1) of Reg. 17/62, the Commission has the power to request the competent authorities of the Member States to undertake the investigations which the Commission considers to be necessary under Art. 14 (1), or which it has ordered by decision pursuant to Art. 14 (3). Thus, it is clear that the Commission might invoke the assistance of national authorities of its Member States and that these authorities might use the remedies available to them to enforce compliance. Although Art. 13 (1) refers mainly to investigations to be carried out by the competent authorities in the Member State in whose territory the investigation is to be made, the powers granted to the Commission are not necessarily limited in this respect. It is not excluded that the Commission might ask the authorities of a Member State to assist it in obtaining information located entirely outside the territory of the Community, and to use their available remedies to this end.

(This issue will be considered more generally under heading 11 – 'Bi- and Multilateral Treaties' – below).

*b) Effects*

The capacity of the Commission to impose periodic penalty payments in the event of a refusal to supply information requested by way of formal decision appears to be the major coercive remedy here.

*c) Letters Rogatory*

Not applicable.

## 6.4 FRANCE

*a) Remedies*

Save in the case of letters rogatory, it is not possible to compel a foreign company to answer any questions directed to it with regard to antitrust matters.

*b) Effects*

If a foreign enterprise is requesting permission for a merger, non-compliance with a request for information on a voluntary basis may result in such permission being denied.

*c) Letters Rogatory*

There is no provision for any remedy available in France to sanction a refusal to comply with an investigation conducted by foreign authorities abroad in response to letters rogatory. The French authorities rely upon the authorities of the requested state employing such remedies as they have available to enforce compliance.

When letters rogatory are sent to French authorities by a foreign government they will be honoured only on the basis of a Treaty.

## 6.5 U.K.

*a) Remedies*

No provision under U.K. law.

*b) Effects*

Not relevant, in the light of the extreme 'territorial' policy adopted by the Office of Fair Trading and the courts.

*c) Letters Rogatory*

Where letters rogatory are submitted to a U.K. court in antitrust matters, the court will do its utmost to assist the requesting court, as outlined by the judges in the Court of Appeal in the *Westinghouse* case. The remedy of contempt will be available against recalcitrant witnesses. However, foreign witnesses are entitled to claim protection from self-incrimination under the Fifth Amendment to the U.S. constitution where the letters rogatory issue from an American court: In *re Westinghouse Electric Corp. Uranium Contracts Litigation* (1978) A.C. 547.

The Protection of Trading Interests Act 1980, by Section 4, provides that 'A court shall not make an order under s. 2 of the Evidence (Proceedings in Other Jurisdictions) Act 1975 ... If it is shown that the request infringes the jurisdiction of the United Kingdom or is otherwise prejudicial to the sovereignty of the United Kingdom.

## 6.6 SWITZERLAND

Given the strictly territorial approach to jurisdiction adopted by the Swiss government and the extreme hostility evidenced in response to assertions of extraterritorial jurisdiction in antitrust matters by the competent authorities of other States, it is not surprising to find that the only means of procedure in Switzerland is by way of letters rogatory which will be honoured on a basis of reciprocity. In effect, Swiss cartel law is strictly confined to Swiss territory and the law on business secrecy effectively prevents the production of information, even voluntarily, for use in foreign antitrust proceedings: see e.g. *the Hoffmann la Roche 'Vitamins' case* before the ECJ and the subsequent Decision of the E.C. Commission in the case of *Adams* (Adams supplied information to the Commission in contravention of Swiss law on business secrecy, was prosecuted in Switzerland and has since, on the recommendation of the European Parliament, received 'compensation' from the E.C. Commission).

## 6.7 ITALY

Not applicable.

## 6.8 AUSTRALIA

### *a) Remedies*

No provision.

### *b) Effects*

Not applicable.

### *c) Letters Rogatory*

There is no provision for any remedy available in Australia to sanction a refusal to comply with an investigation conducted by foreign authorities abroad in response to letters rogatory. The Australian authorities rely upon the authorities of the State to which the letters rogatory were addressed employing such remedies as they have available to enforce compliance.

# 7. Procedures whereby a foreign enterprise may be attacked through purely domestic channels

## 7.0 INTRODUCTION

Quite apart from the nationality principle discussed above which may enable a State to extend its jurisdiction over certain enterprises located abroad, there are various other procedures in certain jurisdictions whereby an undertaking situated abroad may be brought within domestic jurisdiction. As these various procedural methods occur in different national legal systems, it is proposed to examine them on a general basis giving such examples of their existence as lend clarity.

## 7.1 APPOINTMENT OF A DOMICILE WITHIN THE JURISDICTION

Various legal systems provide in certain circumstances for the appointment by national authorities of a domicile for a foreign enterprise within the jurisdiction. This obviates the need to attempt to proceed extraterritorially.

*Germany*

In the case of legalised cartels, (such as specialisation and export cartels) which do not possess their own legal identity, paragraph 36 GWB provides that the cartel is obliged to nominate a representative who is then responsible for answering any questions directed by the BKartA and upon whom documents may be served by the BKartA. This provision applies to domestic and foreign cartels equally. If the cartel refuses to appoint such a representative, the BKartA may ask the local court to appoint such representative without the cooperation of the cartel. This possibility has to date never been employed.

*Switzerland*

The Swiss authorities view as compatible with general principles of international law an informal letter addressed by mail to a party abroad inviting it to appoint a domestic domicile for the purpose of personal service. (*See* e.g. the submission by the Swiss Ambassador to the E.C. Commission in the *Dyestuffs* cases 48/69 and 53/69, where it was suggested that the same rule be applied in the reverse situation).

## 7.2 PUBLIC SERVICE OF PROCESS

A procedure for the public service of process is available in many jurisdictions and may be used where doubts are felt as to the compatibility of extraterritorial service with the principles of public international law. Thus, Germany and the EEC, among others, recognise such an institution. In order to conform with the principle of international law guaranteeing a fair trial, it appears that such a time and venue for public service must be appointed as would reasonably enable the defendant to know the extent of the case against him.

An informal letter sent by ordinary mail notifying the defendant of the provision for public service and of the date upon which he, personally, is to be served by this means, might be an acceptable guarantee of this right and compatible with public international law, (but note the possibility of objection to such a letter by e.g. the Swiss government: *see* 3.1 above).

This provision for public service of process was employed recently in Germany in the Bayer/Firestone case (*see* 4.2.5 above).

## 7.3 THE ENTERPRISE ENTITY DOCTRINE

Under this heading it is proposed to investigate those situations where the presence of an 'arm' of the foreign enterprise pursued within the physical territory of the State under whose law proceedings are sought to be brought is used as a medium for attacking the enterprise abroad.

1) May a) a branch, b) a subsidiary or c) an agent of the enterprise be used as the venue for service of process or as the recipient of requests for information?

2) Does the present of a) a branch, b) a subsidiary or c) an agent within the jurisdiction suffice to found jurisdiction over the enterprise located abroad, even where such a branch, subsidiary or agent was not involved in or party to the restrictive trade practice, merger or joint venture complained of? (This is essentially the personal jurisdiction problem, dealt with under 3.5 above).

The 'enterprise entity' doctrine has been variously expressed. The U.S. Government expressed its view in a memorandum from the U.S. Department of Justice transmitted to the Embassy of Japan, Washington D.C., with a Note of July 3, 1958, as:

> 'When a subsidiary acts on behalf of a foreign parent, and there is such an identity of interest between the two or such control by one over the other that one is in reality the alter ego of the other, or its mere agent, instrumentality, or adjunct, then the parent comes within the U.S. jurisdiction.'
>
> (*See* Whiteman, Digest of International Law, Vol. 6 at 118-19, (1968)).

The European Court of Justice has considered in various cases the question of whether and in what circumstances legally distinct undertakings will be regarded as forming a single economic entity, for the purposes of either Art. 85 or Art. 86, EEC Treaty.

(*See* e.g. *United Brands* Case, *Commercial Solvents* Case etc.)

In Case 48/69, *Imperial Chemical Industries v. Commission* (1972), the European Court said:

> 'The fact that the subsidiary has a distinct legal personality does not suffice to dispose of the possibility that its behaviour might be imputed to the parent company. Such may be the case in particular when the subsidiary, although having a distinct legal personality, does not determine its behaviour on the market in an autonomous manner but essentially carries out the instructions given to it by the parent company.'

Some degree of economic dependence seems to be a common denominator for all such tests, and this principle of economic dependence or control is used to create a fictional legal unity for both substantive and procedural law purposes. This obviously simplifies the task of the cartel authorities, especially in that either national courts or the cartel authorities themselves are able to determine for themselves the required degree of dependency between the foreign enterprise and its domestic 'arm'.

### 7.3.1 The domestic 'arm' as the vehicle for service of process

#### *7.3.1.1 USA*

Under U.S. law, service upon a branch of an enterprise will be effective as service upon the parent company. A branch is by definition not a separate legal entity, but part of the foreign corporation found on domestic territory.

Service of process on a subsidiary would not necessarily constitute service on the parent, but will only do so where the former is held to be the agent of the latter, or the two are held to be a single entity for legal purposes (*see* 5.5 above). There is no generally accepted definition of the word 'agent' as used here. United States courts look to the pattern of conduct of the subsidiary to determine whether it is conducting its own business or is merely acting as an agent for its parent. (*See* e.g., *Frummer v. Hilton Hotels International, Inc.*, 19 N.Y. 2d 533, 227 N.E. 2d 851, 281 NYS 2d 41, *cert. denied*, 389 U.S. 923 (1967) (Jurisdiction over owner of foreign hotel by service on U.S. subsidiary which accepted room reservations for the foreign hotel). Rule 4 (d) (3) Fed. R. Civ. P. provides that service of process upon a domestic or foreign corporation is to be made by 'delivering a copy of the summons and of the complaint to an officer, a managing or general agent, or to any other agent authorised by appointment or by law to receive service of process ...' Thus, certain categories of agents are capable of service.

### 7.3.1.2 *Germany*

The legal provisions about service of process do not provide for the general possibility of serving documents on the German subsidiary and/or affiliate and/or agent of a foreign company. According to paragraph 8 VwZG and paragraphs 36 sub paragraph 1 and 57 sub paragraph 1 sentence 2 GWB the German antitrust authorities may serve documents only to such persons in Germany who have been appointed by the foreign enterprise for this purpose and are in possession of a power of attorney. This power of attorney need not be a special power of attorney, but may be a general power to represent the foreign company in Germany, including representation in administrative proceedings. Persons having a 'general power of attorney' or who are authorised 'signatories' in the meaning of German commercial law (Prokurist) or who have a commercial authority in the meaning of German commercial law (Handlungsbevollmächtigter) are generally deemed to have the power of attorney to receive documents in a formal service of process. However, such power of attorney cannot be presumed in the case of legal representatives of a German subsidiary or affiliate or branch, let alone in the case of independent agents. Their power of attorney is limited and restricted to the business of the German subsidiary or affiliate or the German branch and – in the case of independent agents – to the carrying out of the business as defined by the agency agreement. Although the details are very controversial, the question whether a person has a power of attorney to act for a foreign enterprise must be defined according to the general principles of civil and commercial law. Apart from an express power of attorney, therefore, the power may also result from tolerating acts of the German representatives of the foreign company even where they possess no formal power of attorney (Duldungsvollmacht) (e.g. where the representative accepts letters for the foreign company for a certain period of time, with the knowledge of that company).

It cannot be said, therefore, that the theory of 'enterprise entity' is accepted by German law with regard to the matter of service of process. Service of process upon German subsidiaries, affiliates, branches or the independent agents of foreign enterprises is not generally possible.

Such service of process would be valid only if the person or enterprise could be proved to have a power of attorney pertaining to such service of process granted by the foreign enterprise.

Although the German antitrust authorities have tried in certain cases to serve documents formally upon German representatives, in some cases they did not insist upon the validity of such service after the German representative had pointed out that he had no power of attorney to receive such documents.

### 7.3.1.3 *EEC*

The European Court of Justice in the ALMA decision, ruled that when the document to be served reached the internal sphere of the addressee the service was sufficient.

On the basis of this general rule it seems that the requirements of EEC law would be met where process is served upon a foreign company through a controlled subsidiary. In the *Dyestuffs* cases, with regard to the companies located outside the EEC, the Commission notified its decision to their subsidiaries within the Community, stating that, since those subsidiaries were wholly controlled by their parent companies, they were within the internal structure of those parent companies.

The Court rejected the applicant's contention that the notification was irregular and stated that, as the applicants had obtained full knowledge of the decision and exercised their rights to institute proceedings within the prescribed period, the question of irregularity of notification was irrelevant.

Notification through a branch should raise no difficulty, for a branch is in form a part of the foreign company which depends for its existence upon the company's existence.

The notification to an independent agent within the Community should not in general be considered to meet the requirement of service of process. As mentioned above, (see point 4.3.5 above), Article 191 requires that 'decisions shall be notified to those to whom they are addressed and shall take effect upon such notification'. An independent agent could not normally be considered to be within the *'sphère interne'* of the foreign company, even though there is a tendency in EEC substantive laws to consider independent agents, in certain conditions, to be within the 'economic unit'. It would seem that only if the independent agent had a specific obligation to inform the foreign country of such notification, either because he had been specifically appointed as the representative of the foreign company in its dealings with the EEC authorities or because the agent was the general legal representative of the foreign company within the Community, would it be possible to consider that service had been duly made on the party to whom the decision was addressed. This is why, in question I.6 in Form A/B the Commission requires one to state the name and address of a representative within the Community.

### *7.3.1.4 France*

As the independent legal entity of a subsidiary is respected by French law, service of process in administrative proceedings could not be made on a subsidiary, even one which was fully owned. The general rule of the Code of Civil Procedure is that service of process must be made upon 'the person' (by which is meant the legal representative of a company) or upon such persons as have been appointed for this purpose. Thus, it is doubtful whether service of process made upon a branch or independent agent is valid where such branch or agent has not been duly appointed.

In criminal proceedings (Art. 419, and Art. 50 when the case has been transmitted to the criminal authorities) service of process may only be made upon the foreign physical person incriminated (i.e. the Chairman of the Board or the responsible officers of a foreign enterprise).

### *7.3.1.5 U.K.*

U.K. law regards a branch as a part of the parent company established upon national territory and thus service of process upon a branch would suffice for service upon the parent company.

As a general rule, the separate legal personality of parent and subsidiary companies is respected under U.K. law. Thus, service upon a subsidiary would not be effective as service upon its parent.

Service upon an agent will only be sufficient where that agent is endowed with authority to accept such service on behalf of the parent enterprise, i.e. where the agent has legal power to enter into contracts on behalf of its principal.

### *7.3.1.6 Switzerland*

The physical presence within the jurisdiction constitutes the relevant point of attachment to justify the assumption of jurisdiction for the opening of adminstrative procedures. Much therefore depends upon the definition of this term, but no express rules exist with regard to the definition of that presence with regard to a foreign enterprise's subsidiary, branch or agent.

By comparative analysis with other fields of international administrative law, the following conclusions may be suggested:

Proper service on a branch, with effect for the foreign parent, requires that a substantive link between the branch and the violation of substantive law notified to the branch of a foreign party must exist.

This substantive law element also determines to what extent an agent may constitute a sufficient point of attachment to justify proper service on the foreign principal. As a rule, the independent agent will not constitute a permanent establishment of the foreign principal, as business is transacted and closed for the risk of the principal but in the agent's own name.

The independent legal entity of a subsidiary is respected by Swiss law, even in the event of full control by a foreign parent and economic identity. Therefore, service on the subsidiary on behalf of the foreign parent would only be proper if the subsidiary were appointed as domicile for the purpose of accepting service on behalf of the parent (*see* 7.1 above).

### *7.3.1.7 Italy*

For the purpose of comparison, it is interesting to note that, under the general rules of civil procedure, service upon an Italian branch of a foreign enterprise is regarded as good service upon the enterprise, unless the authority to receive service has been specifically excluded from the powers granted to the representative of the branch.

Service upon a subsidiary or agent will not be valid unless the foreign person or company has made an election of domicile in Italy.

*7.3.1.8 Australia*

If a corporation wishes to conduct business in any State of the Commonwealth, it is necessary for that corporation to be registered as a foreign corporation within one month after it establishes a place of business or commences trading within the State. Once a corporation is registered, any process may be served upon it by registered post directed to the registered office. The Commissioner for Corporate Affairs maintains a list of the registered offices, and a search can be readily obtained. Therefore, the question of serving a foreign corporation causes no problem.

# 8. Contesting the jurisdiction of national courts or antitrust authorities

## 8.0 INTRODUCTION

One very important procedural question here is whether it is possible for a defendant to an antitrust action to appear before a court or administrative agency in order to contest the jurisdiction of that body over him in the case concerned, without running the risk of thereby being held to have submitted himself to that jurisdiction.

In this context, it is perhaps appropriate to mention a similar problem which has arisen in certain proceedings before the E.C. Commission. In such proceedings, the Commission has, on occasion, argued that the simple act of filing an agreement with the Commission, or of consenting to participation in an agreement being mentioned in the application for a negative clearance or exemption *by a third party*, may be held to constitute a submission to the jurisdiction of the Commission. (For details, *see* 3.5.1 above).

## 8.1 AUSTRALIA

In Australia, an appearance before the Federal Court can be conditional and this is so where the respondent corporation objects to the jurisdiction. The respondent is able to argue this point without consenting to the full jurisdiction of the Court.

## 8.2 U.K.

Service of process out of the jurisdiction is provided for under Order 11 of the Rules of the Supreme Court (1965). An order granting leave to serve a writ or notice or a writ out of the jurisdiction must be obtained from the Court and must limit a time within which the defendant to be served must make an appearance (Order 11, Rule 4).

An unconditional appearance is a submission to the jurisdiction, and therefore waives any objection to the order under which service is made. After service, the defendant may apply to set aside the order or service without making an appearance (*see Boyle v. Sacker* (1888) 39 Ch. D. 249). To avoid a judgment in default of appearance, it is customary to enter with leave a conditional appearance (Order 12, Rule 7).

If a defendant not only objects to service but also takes any step to have the plaintiff's case decided on the merits, he will, if his objection fails, have submitted to the jurisdiction. The same consequence will follow the entry of a conditional appearance in the ordinary form, which provides that the appearance is to stand as unconditional if the application to set aside fails. The safest course is therefore to apply under Order 12, Rule 8, without entering any appearance at all and to confine the application strictly to the discharge of the ex parte order for service and to any irregularity in service.

## 8.3 USA

In the United States, an appearance in a court to contest the issue of jurisdiction can be made without that appearance itself being deemed a basis upon which jurisdiction can be established (Fed. R. Civ. P. 12).

# 9. Enforcement of national judgments, acts or decisions of national antitrust authorities abroad

## 9.0 INTRODUCTION

It is necessary to distinguish those situations where antitrust authorities have independent authority to impose fines or issue cease and desist orders, which then take effect directly and are not required to be issued through the authority of a court (e.g. EEC, Germany), from those where antitrust agencies proceed through the medium of the courts in acting against the antitrust violators (e.g., USA, U.K.). Different again are those systems which rely partly upon private actions brought by individuals for the enforcement of antitrust law provisions (e.g. USA, Switzerland). In the first situation described there may well be appeal procedures before the courts, as indeed there are in the two jurisdictions cited as examples.

The distinction is important insofar as enforcement outside the jurisdiction of administrative authorities' decisions may well be more difficult than the enforcement of court judgments, because few treaties for the reciprocal enforcement of administrative decisions exist.

## 9.1 USA

There are no reported instances of acts or decisions of U.S. antitrust authorities being enforced outside the United States. However, many cases brought by the U.S. government are settled by agreements between the government and the defendant which must be approved by the judge who has jurisdiction over the case. If the judge approves the agreement, it is entered as an order of the court. Consequently, violation of such an order may result in the imposition of penalties for contempt of court.

Such 'consent decree' agreements often contain clauses providing that foreign defendants will take, or will refrain from taking, certain actions outside the U.S. A saving clause is frequently included which provides that nothing in the decree shall compel a violation of foreign law.

## 9.2 GERMANY

No formal decisions or other acts of sovereignty of the German antitrust authorities have ever been enforced outside Germany. Enforcement or execution would constitute an act of sovereignty, which would need the consent of the foreign State prior to implementation.

In the case of an *International Cartel of Producers of Lightning Conductor Wire*, the BKartA in its press release – No. 37/78 of August 14, 1978 – mentioned that this was the first case in which it had made use of the possibility of imposing fines on foreign (Austrian) participants in the cartel, although they did not maintain any branches, agents, subsidiaries etc. in Germany. However, the Austrian enterprises, informed by the BKartA by ordinary mail of the proceedings, appointed a common attorney to represent them in the proceedings and have since paid the fines voluntarily, without any subsequent compulsory execution being necessary.

In the recent *Casting Roller* case where the foreign companies involved received administrative fine decisions they did not appeal and seem to have paid the fines imposed.

In the *Scandinavian Paper Case*, the BKartA indicated its view that administrative fines may also be executed against foreign defendants by seizing the property of the German subsidiaries of the foreign enterprises, as these subsidiaries and their parent companies formed an 'economic unity'. The issue was never decided, for the file was closed without a decision.

It is interesting to note that the BKartA is of the opinion that compulsory execution could be effected against the property of the German subsidiaries directly without it being necessary first to seize the shares of these subsidiaries.

### 9.3 EEC

No enforcement of any Commission decision or of any judgment of the European Court of Justice has been attempted outside the territory of the Community. Nevertheless, enterprises located abroad have performed acts outside the Community as a result of such decisions.

### 9.4 FRANCE

No act or decision of French antitrust authorities has ever been enforced outside French territory.

### 9.5 U.K.

No act or decision of the U.K. antitrust authorities has ever been enforced outside the territory of the U.K.

### 9.6 SWITZERLAND

The scope of the enforcement jurisdiction in administrative matters is limited to strict territoriality.

## 9.7 ITALY

Not applicable

## 9.8 AUSTRALIA

The Trade Practices Act does not set out the enforcement proceedings to be taken once judgment is given. In this regard, the States have enacted legislation dealing with the enforcement and recognition of judgments. There is no equivalent federal legislation.

In practice, no decisions under the Trade Practices Act have been enforced outside the territory. However, cases do exist where informal assistance between antitrust authorities has led to the cessation of activities in breach of the Trade Practices Act. For example, where a German company sent invoices or what purported to be invoices to telex users in Australia notifying them that they could be included in an international telex directory, this was held to be 'misleading conduct' and to constitute an offence under the Trade Practices Act. The company was not within the jurisdiction, but, by approaching the German government, the Trade Practices Commission ensured that legal action was taken by that Government against the companies concerned and action that was in breach of the Trade Practices Act ceased. Such assistance was, however, based on international comity, and not the result of any formal agreement.

## 9.9 THE ICI-CASE

It is now appropriate to consider in more detail one of the most important U.S. decisions attempting to enforce U.S. antitrust law abroad, and also to consider the means of enforcement available to the civil litigant, rather than the State authority, who has a judgment in his favour against a foreign respondent, say in a suit for treble damages under the Sherman Act.

The *ICI* case perhaps best illustrates the conflicts which may arise between two sovereign jurisdictions where orders are made by one court directing the conduct of the defendant outside that court's jurisdiction.

*United States v. Imperial Chemical Industries, Limited*, 105 F, Supp. 215 (SDNY 1952) (the 'ICI' case)

In this case, the U.S. District Court found that du Pont and ICI had joined in a conspiracy to restrain trade in chemical products by dividing world markets through the use of patents and patent licences. After the litigation had begun, du Pont assigned its British patents to ICI in an apparent attempt to thwart any impending judgment that would adversely affect du Pont's patent rights. To prevent this evasion, the U.S. court ordered ICI to reassign the British patent rights against imported goods licensed under corresponding U.S. patents.

The American judge stated that:

> [T]he effectiveness of the exercise of that power depends upon the recognition which will be given to our judgment as a matter of comity by the courts of the foreign sovereign which has granted the patents in question.

Id. at 229. ICI argued that it could not comply with the judge's order because it had granted irrevocable and exclusive licences under the British patents to another British company, British Nylon Spinners Ltd, ('BNS'). Although BNS was not a party to the U.S. litigation, and, therefore was not subject to the court's jurisdiction *in personam*, the judge rejected ICI's argument because BNS was fifty per cent owned by ICI and was, therefore, not an uninvolved party. Moreover, he found that BNS's rights under the licences were 'wholly subject to the inherent vices of the agreements through which they were acquired.' Ibid at 231. The judge added that BNS was free to challenge the order in English courts and that those courts could decide whether to recognise the validity of the order as a matter of comity.

Within two weeks of the issuance of the district court's order BNS obtained an injunction in an English court restraining ICI from complying with the U.S. decree and ordering specific performance of the ICI-BNS contract. In affirming the interlocutory injunction against ICI, the English Chancery Court of Appeal questioned whether, notwithstanding principles of comity, the U.S. order was such an unacceptable assertion of extraterritorial jurisdiction that English courts could not recognise it. The English judges took the position that considerations of comity should have restrained the American court from asserting extraterritorial jurisdiction in the first place.

An interesting additional aspect of this case is referred to by Neale as illustrating how, even when exercise of jurisdiction is difficult to fault on technical grounds, the consequences of decrees with influence on foreign trade may be far reaching and produce disadvantageous effects on innocent third parties, leading to State protest. (A. Neale, *The Antitrust Laws of the USA* 367 (2d ed. 1970).)

In the ICI case, one part of the court's order directed the termination of joint ownerships by the two companies of certain foreign concerns. Among these was Canadian Industries Limited, in which ICI and du Pont each held 42% of the stock, the balance being held by Canadians. The management was mainly Canadian. The Canadian's position was strategically good and provided a balancing effect upon the two major stockholders. 'The effect of the Court's decree was to require either ICI or du Pont to dispose of their holdings but it did not prevent one or other from acquiring the whole 84%. The order might therefore profoundly affect Canadian interests in the concern.' Ibid at 372.

## 9.10 GENERAL REMARKS

In the U.S., where an important part of antitrust enforcement is represented by civil suits brought by private parties complaining of damage incurred as a result of anticompetitive pactices, the question of how such judgments are to be enforced introduces a new dimension to the debate, which does not arise in any of the other jurisdictions considered here save, potentially, in Switzerland.

If the foreign defendant possesses assets within the U.S. territory, then the traditional methods of attachment, garnishment and contempt are available to enforce compliance with any judgment. Problems may arise where a foreign-based corporation is the defendant, and has no 'assets' other than a wholly-owned subsidiary within the U.S. A few cases exist where demonstration that the parent owned all the capital stock of a subsidiary and that the officers were identical was held to indicate that there was no real diversity of interest and to render attachment possible. The majority of decisions, however, support the view that these factors are not sufficient to justify attachment, and that some indication of the subsidiary's having been used for an improper purpose and of its being under the actual control of the parent must be present (E. Kintner & M. Joelson, *An International Antitrust Primer* 59 (1974).)

## 9.11 ENFORCEMENT BY INSTITUTION OF A NEW ACTION IN THE COURT WITH JURISDICTION OVER THE DEFENDANT

The plaintiff seeking to enforce a judgment against a foreign defendant may also attempt to institute a new action in the courts of the foreign state with jurisdiction over the defendant. There are no general principles regarding mutual recognition of judgments, but rather a plethora of unilateral, bilateral and multilateral arrangements governing the area. Most nations act in accordance with a rule of reciprocity, but the difficulties inherent in establishing the extent to which a judgment issuing in one legal system is given effect within another legal system render this principle extremely complicated in operation. Most States refuse anyway to recognise judgments that are penal in nature or contrary to the public policy of the State before whose courts enforcement is sought. Thus, in many jurisdictions, judgments for treble damages would not be enforced, being regarded as penal in nature. (*See* Lord Wilberforce in the *Westinghouse* case).

# 10. Defence of State Sovereignty in Antitrust Matters

## 10.1 BY STATE PROTEST

Since 1945, at least twenty foreign governments have protested American assertions of jurisdiction in international antitrust cases.

Similarly, the E.C. Commission has met with hostile reactions from other national authorities when attempting to apply its antitrust laws extraterritorially (e.g. Aide Memoire of British Government in the *Dyestuffs* case, 1969, and the refusal of the Swiss Ambassador to forward notification of the decision in that case to a subsidiary of the Swiss companies involved established with the Common Market).

## 10.2 BY THE NATIONAL COURTS

The *ICI* case described above is an excellent illustration of how national courts may react to protest against infringements of State Sovereignty by foreign antitrust authorities or assertions of jurisdiction by foreign courts.

## 10.3 BY THE ENACTMENT OF LEGISLATION

The strength of feeling against such wide-reaching interpretations of antitrust jurisdiction as that of the U.S. government and courts is plainly expressed in the volume of 'blocking legislation' enacted by various States in the post-war years to protect against assertions of such jurisdiction, and/or to preclude compliance with discovery orders issued by U.S. courts for testimony and documents outside the United States. See e.g. Foreign Antitrust Act No. 13 1979, and Protection of Trading Interests Act, U.K. 1980.

### 10.3.1 USA

The U.S. has no such laws for the protection of its citizens against actions of foreign antitrust authorities, as is to be expected in a State which is attempting to convince its major trading partners of the crucial importance of active antitrust controls.

### 10.3.2 Germany

Germany has no law comparable to the U.K. Protection of Trading Interests Act, 1980, affording protection to German citizens or enterprises against actions of foreign antitrust authorities.

On one occasion, in connection with the U.S. antitrust activities against the international freight conferences in the sixties, Germany reacted by altering paragraph 11 of the statute relating to the Powers of the German Federal Authorities in the Field of the Merchant Marine to the extent that the Federal Minister for Communications was empowered to issue a regulation prohibiting the production or disclosure of documents referring to the merchant marine (especially contracts, statistics, opinions) and any answers to requests for information by foreign authorities, or to introduce the requirement of permission of the Minister for such acts. This power may be exercised only if it is necessary in order to protect the German merchant marine and its commercial freedom.

The Federal Minister for Communications has used this power to issue a regulation of December 14, 1966, according to which any disclosure of documents to or the answering of a request for information from a foreign authority needs the permission of the Federal Minister.

In extraordinary cases, in which foreign antitrust authorities might try to collect information or carry out searches in Germany pretending to act by authorisation of a German authority this would be a violation of German criminal law (paragraph 132 StGB). German industry, however, is strongly demanding protective legislation similar to the U.K. Protection of Trading Interests Act 1980. (*See* 10.3.5 below).

### 10.3.3 EEC

In a letter sent by Dr. Schlieder, Director General of the Directorate General of Competition (IV) of the Commission, in February 1978, to Mr. Shenefield, his counterpart in the U.S. Department of Justice, he stated that:

> '[T]he problems which would arise from the application of American antitrust legislation (to) enterprises (in the Common Market) concern the sovereignty of Member States.'

No provision exists under EEC law for protection of Community nationals or residents against actions of foreign antitrust authorities.

### 10.3.4 France

Under a French statute of 16th July 1980, it is prohibited to any French person or legal entity to communicate to any foreign public authority documents or information of economic, commercial, industrial, financial or technical nature, where such communication may affect the sovereignty security and the essential economic interests of France.

Likewise, it is prohibited to any person to ask for or to communicate such documents or information as might constitute evidence for use in foreign proceedings, either judicial or administrative.

The provisions of this statute of 16th July 1980 are criminal in nature (with penalties ranging from two to six months' imprisonment) and are not specifically restricted to antitrust proceedings.

The French statute is not as broad as the British Protection of Trading Interests Act 1980, for it was passed, for constitutional reasons, as an amendment to an existing statute which dealt with maritime and aviation matters (of July 26th 1968) because the matter was urgent. However, during the debate the Minister informed Parliament that the government was preparing a new statute to cover the other matters dealt with in the British Act and that a new statute would be presented to Parliament in the spring of 1981.

### 10.3.5 U.K.

A foreign judgment cannot be enforced in England without the institution of fresh legal proceedings either to register the judgment as an English judgment, under the Foreign Judgments (Reciprocal Enforcement) Act 1933 or the similar 1920 legislation covering certain Commonwealth countries, or at common law in a fresh action based on the foreign judgment. The defendant may then, in either instance, argue in defence that the foreign court in question had no jurisdiction over him.

Where the U.S. Federal Maritime Commission required information to be supplied to it by British Shipping lines, relating to the fixing of rates on the N. Atlantic shipping routes as part of the 'liner conference' system, the U.K. reacted by enacting the Shipping Contracts and Commercial Documents Act 1964 (now repealed) which empowered the U.K. Government to forbid a British Company to supply the information out of the jurisdiction.

The most recent instance of protective legislation enacted by the U.K. Government arose out of the *Westinghouse* proceedings in the United States. In the course of these proceedings, an American judge issued letters rogatory to the English High Court requesting that a British company, Rio Tinto Zinc, should be required to answer certain interrogatories, produce documents and to order certain of its officers to be examined by a U.S. consul in England. In the event, the High Court decided that it could not give effect to letters rogatory in circumstances prejudicial to the sovereignty of the United Kingdom, as was the case here.

The *Westinghouse* litigation, followed by a subsequent case in which a U.S. grand jury handed down criminal indictments for violation of U.S. antitrust law against certain shipping companies including two consortia in which there was a substantial British element, and against two British nationals, alleging that they had established shipping rates without the approval of the U.S. Federal Maritime Commission, led the U.K. Government to introduce a Bill in the autumn of 1979 which was enacted on 20th March 1980 as the Protection of Trading Interests Act 1980 (*See* Appendix 3).

The Act is not specifically restricted to antitrust proceedings but in its general power extends more widely to measures taken under the law of any overseas country 'for regulating or controlling international trade' where, insofar as they apply to things done outside that country by persons carrying on business in the U.K., they 'are damaging to the trading interests of the United Kingdom' (s. 1).

The Act generally applies to actions directed by a foreign court or agency to a person or corporation carrying on business within the U.K. (a 'U.K. person') and/or a U.K. citizen or company incorporated in the U.K. (a 'U.K. national'). It covers a number of situations.

*(a) Notification (s. 1)*

A U.K. person may be required to notify the Secretary of State of 'any requirements or prohibition imposed' on him under such an overseas measure.

*(b) Non-compliance with foreign order (s. 1(3))*

A U.K. person may be forbidden by the Secretary of State to comply with such a foreign order, if the latter thinks it appropriate 'for avoiding damage to the trading interests of the U.K.'.

*(c) Supply of information (s. 2)*

The Secretary of State may forbid (specifically or generally) a U.K. person to produce to any foreign authority commercial documents or commercial information which is not within the territorial jurisdiction of the foreign country or to comply with a foreign order to publish it, if

'(a) it infringes the jurisdiction of the U.K. or is otherwise prejudicial to the sovereignty of the U.K.; or

(b) compliance with the requirement would be prejudicial to the security of the U.K. or to the relations of the government of the U.K. with the government of any other country; or

(c) it is made otherwise than for the purposes of civil or criminal proceedings which have been instituted in the overseas country; or

(d) it requires a person to state what documents relevant to any such proceedings are or have been in his possession, custody or power or to produce for the purposes of any proceedings any documents other than particular documents specified in the requirement.'

*(d) Letters rogatory*

A request made to a U.K. court to take evidence on behalf of a foreign court under s. 2 of the Evidence (Proceedings in Other Jurisdictions) Act 1975 shall not be complied with 'if it is shown that the request infringes the jurisdiction of the United Kingdom or is otherwise prejudicial to the sovereignty of the United Kingdom' or if the Secretary of State so certifies.

*(e) Multiple damages (ss. 5 and 6)*

No foreign judgment awarding multiple damages shall be enforceable in the U.K. nor shall a foreign judgment based on a law which appears to the Secretary of State 'to be concerned with the prohibition or regulation of agreements, arrangements or practices designed to restrain, distort or restrict competition in the carrying on of business of any description or to be otherwise concerned with the promotion of such competition'. Where multiple damages have been awarded abroad against a U.K. national or U.K. person (except where he was ordinarily resident in the foreign country, or carried on business there and the judgment was concerned with activities exclusively carried on there), and he has paid them whether voluntarily or by forced execution, he may recover in the U.K. courts from the successful plaintiff the excess damages, i.e. that part in excess of what represents simple compensation.

The last provision is the most original and reflects the concern felt by the British Government and business circles at the penal consequences of multiple damages (parallel to a similar concern at the high penal damages awarded by U.S. courts in products liability cases).

It is interesting that even in this very strong assertion of U.K. territorial jurisdiction the limitations of that jurisdiction are accepted. A penalty is provided against persons who fail to comply with an order of the Secretary of State (e.g. who supply documents to the foreign agency when the Secretary of State has forbidden them to). But the penalty does not apply to a non-U.K. national for anything done outside the U.K. (even if that person is carrying on business or is resident in the U.K.). The U.K. is thus maintaining its strict attitude to territorial jurisdiction over acts within the territory and personal jurisdiction over its own nationals.

### 10.3.6 Switzerland

Although Switzerland has no specific legal provisions for protecting its citizens and companies against actions of foreign administrative agencies, there are a series of provisions in its penal system which contribute to establishing such protection.

Art. 273 of the Swiss Penal Code provides that whoever makes inquiries about a manufacturing or business secret in order to make it accessible to a foreign official authority or to a foreign organisation or to a private enterprise or to its agents shall be exposed to penal sanctions. This provision was applied in the Adams case. Adams submitted information protected by Art. 273 to the E.C. Commission in the Hoffmann La Roche Case, in which considerable fines were imposed on Hoffmann for violation of EEC antitrust law.

Art. 271 of the Code provides that whoever acts on Swiss territory without permission, on behalf of a foreign State, in a manner reserved to a public authority or civil servant shall be exposed to penal sanctions. This is directed at actions which, in their subject matter, are reserved to the State. It is immaterial whether the offender is a civil servant of a foreign State acting in an official capacity or is acting as a private person.

The sanction is also available to penalise an abuse of investigating rights derived from a treaty e.g. rights provided regarding judicial assistance in criminal cases used to carry out investigations in a fiscal matter.

According to the Federal Department of Justice and Police, letters of a foreign authority addressed directly to a Swiss resident, as well as direct service of documents, by-passing the customary diplomatic channels of transmission, are regarded as an interference with Swiss sovereignty and punishable under Art. 271.

The Swiss law on banking secrecy, supplementary to the general rule of Art. 321 of the Penal Code protecting, by way of penal sanctions, professional secrets of professionals such as doctors, lawyers etc., will grant the account holder, whether resident in Switzerland or abroad, full protection against inquiries by foreign States or organisations.

### 10.3.7 Italy

Article 802 of the Code of Civil Procedure provides that requests from foreign judicial authorities for the examination of witnesses, technical experts, interrogatories or other evidence are to be submitted for *exequatur* to the Court of Appeals of the place where the evidence must be taken, after having heard the opinion of the District Attorney. If the Court of Appeals grants the *exequatur*, the request is forwarded to the competent judge.

An *exequatur* will not be granted if the request is deemed to conflict with Italian public policy. While it is not known of any such request by foreign Antitrust Authorities, it is conceivable that the issue of public policy might be raised if the action of such Authorities conflicts with an Italian governmental interest or an applicable Italian economic interest.

There is some controversy as to whether Italian courts will honour requests involving the use of procedures for obtaining evidence which are not recognised by Italian procedural law.

It is also to be noted that Article 249 of the Code of Civil Procedure extends to witnesses in civil cases the privilege provided for by Article 351 and 352 of the Code of Criminal Procedure, according to which attorneys, physicians, ministers, public officials and public employees cannot be compelled to disclose information which they have received in connection with their professional activities.

By an Act (no. 488) of the 24th July 1980, there is now legislation to prohibit Italian shipowners from supplying to foreign authorities documents and information concerning maritime activities. Sanctions are provided for by the Act. (An unofficial translation may be found in Appendix 3).

### 10.3.8 Australia

Following the *Westinghouse* decision of the United States Court, the Commonwealth enacted the Foreign Antitrust Judgments (Restriction of Enforcement) Act 1979. This is an act containing only three sections which provides, inter alia, in Section 3 (2) where 'the Attorney General is satisfied that:

(i) The Court in giving that judgment exercised a jurisdiction or powers of a kind or in a manner inconsistent with international law or comity and the recognition or enforcement of the Judgment in Australia, could or might be detrimental to, or adversely affect, trade or commerce with other countries, the trading operations of a trading or financial corporation formed within the limits of the Commonwealth or any other matters with respect to which the parliament has power to make laws or to which the executive powers of the Commonwealth relate or;

(ii) It is desirable for the purpose of protecting the national interest in relation to trade or commerce with other countries, the trading operations or trading or financial corporation formed within the limits of the Commonwealth or any other matters with respect to which the parliament has power to make laws or to which the executive powers of the Commonwealth relate that the Judgment should not be recognised or enforceable in whole or in part in Australia, the Attorney General may in the case of any Judgment by Order in writing declare that the Judgment shall not be recognised or enforceable in Australia.

This Act was assented to on 15th March 1979. An order under the Act was made on 6th June 1979. This Order was in respect of two Judgments obtained by Westinghouse Electric Corporation and entered by the U.S. District Court on 3rd and 24th January 1979. The Attorney General made the Order under Section 3 because he was satisfied that it was desirable in protection of the national interest 'in relation to the trading operations of trading and financial corporations formed within the limits of the Commonwealth' that the Judgment should not be recognised or enforceable in whole or in part within Australia. He also stated at the time of making the Order: 'the consequences could be of such an order that the very ability of those corporations to maintain their Australian operations would be endangered ... It is in the national interest that their ability to continue those operations be protected from such a liability under a law of a foreign State.' The Attorney General further stated that each of the Judgments should not be recognised or enforceable in Australia.

(See also here the 'Foreign Proceedings (Prohibition of Certain Evidence) Act 1976, described under 3.4.8 above).

In September 1980 an article in the Financial Times newspaper reported that the Australian government 'may soon stiffen its [Australia's] defences against U.S. antitrust judgments involving the payment of multiple damages by Australian companies ... No details of the likely nature of any Australian legislation have been given, although the Government is known to have been thinking for some time of introducing legislation along the lines of the U.K. Protection of Trading Interests Act.'

### 10.3.9 Netherlands

Under the Dutch *Act on Economic Competition* ('Wet Economische Mededinging') which dates back to 1956, it is prohibited to comply with measures or decisions of other States, which relate to rules on competition, to economic dominant positions or to restrictive practices (art. 39). Exemption from this prohibition may be granted upon request by the Dutch Minister of Economic Affairs, who is the competent minister for the application of the Act. Such exemption may be granted subject to conditions.

It is an economic criminal offence for undertakings to act without explicit prior exemption from the Minister. The penalty may, depending on the circumstances, be rather severe, ranging from a fine imposed on the undertaking concerned to imprisonment of the responsible board members or persons involved.

'Measures of other States' include decisions of foreign courts. Measures taken by supranational institutions (e.g. the European Commission) fall outside the scope of this article.

The exemption is generally granted if the compliance with foreign 'antitrust measures' does not run contrary to the Netherlands antitrust policy. It may even be conceivable that in certain cases it may be desirable for the Dutch Government to coordinate its antitrust policy with that of other States.

The case law of art. 39 of the Act shows that so far only requests for compliance with measures related to U.S. antitrust proceedings have been dealt with. The usual form under which art. 39 plays a role, is that Dutch undertakings are asked to answer questions in U.S. antitrust matters before either a Grand Jury, a sub-committee of Congress, the Federal Maritime Board or, simply, the Anti-Trust Division of the Justice Department. In one case, in 1976, three directors of a Dutch undertaking were sub-poenaed to appear in person before a U.S. tribunal to give oral evidence.

In all cases published, permission to comply with the request was granted, albeit that in the last case mentioned the condition was imposed that the evidence should only relate to facts, behaviour and circumstances within the USA[1]

### 10.3.10 Canada

The text of a Bill which was given its first reading on July 11, 1980, in the House of Commons is annexed as Appendix 5. The Bill concerned 'An Act to authorise the making of orders relating to the production of records and the

1. Information on the Dutch situation supplied by Floris Vogelaar, The Hague.

giving of information for the purposes of proceedings in foreign tribunals and in respect of the recognition and enforcement in Canada of certain foreign judgments obtained in antitrust proceedings.' It is expected that the government will proceed with the legislation with a view to enactment in the next several months.

# 11. Bilateral and Multilateral Treaties providing for assistance in border-crossing antitrust investigations

## 11.1 MULTILATERAL TREATIES

It is proposed to examine here first multilateral conventions which might be of assistance to either an administrative agency or private litigant attempting to obtain discovery in an antitrust proceeding, and then to turn to bilateral treaties in which the jurisdictions here concerned are participants.

### 11.1.1 Hague Convention on the service abroad of judicial and extra-judicial documents in civil or commercial matters. Done at the Hague, November 15, 1965

States parties: Barbados, Belgium, Botswana, Denmark, Egypt, Finland, *France, Federal Republic of Germany*, Israel, Japan, Luxembourg, Malawi, Netherlands, Norway, Portugal, Sweden, Turkey, *United Kingdom, United States*.

This convention will only be of assistance in antitrust proceedings and investigations insofar as these may be designated as 'civil or commercial matters'. In the *Westinghouse* proceedings before the English House of Lords, where this concept came under discussion in the context of the Convention on the Taking of Evidence Abroad in Civil or Commercial Matters (for further details see below at 11.1.2), their Lordships designated the American Grand Jury procedure as criminal in nature, and, therefore, not eligible for judicial aid under that Convention. The designation of various types of procedure, originating in various legal systems, must be fraught with difficulty, but it might be reasonable to suppose that States hostile to extraterritorial jurisdiction in antitrust matters will exclude such investigations from their understanding of the term 'civil and commercial matters'. This discussion will be continued in consideration of the Evidence Convention.

The provisions of Article 10 of the Convention are of particular interest in the light of the objections lodged by many States parties to the Convention under the provision in Article $21_2$ (a). Article 10 states:

Provided that the State of destination does not object, the present Convention shall not interfere with:

a) the freedom to send judicial documents, by postal channels, directly to persons abroad;

b) the freedom of judicial officers, officials or other competent persons of the State of origin to effect service of judicial documents directly through the judicial officers, officials or other competent persons of the State of destination.

c) the freedom of any person interested in a judicial proceeding to effect service of judicial documents directly through the judicial officers, officials or other competent persons of the state of destination.

The French government lodged no objection to these provisions; the German government stated that, 'service pursuant to Art. 10 shall not be effected'; the U.K. government provided that, 'with reference to the provisions of paragraphs (b) and (c) of Art. 10, ... documents for service through official channels will be accepted in the U.K. only by the central or additional authorities and only from judicial consular or diplomatic officers of other Contracting States'; the United States Government lodged no objection.

Article 80 of the Convention provides:

> 'Each contracting State shall be free to effect service of judicial documents upon persons abroad, without application of any compulsion, directly through its diplomatic or consular agents.
>
> Any State may declare that it is opposed to such service within its territory, unless the document is to be served upon a national of the State in which the documents originate.'

France and Germany lodged such declarations, the United States and United Kingdom did not.

It must be emphasised, however, that these observations may only be regarded as significant in relationships between the States parties to the Convention. They do not in any way influence the position regarding service of documents issuing from non-party States.

### 11.1.2 Hague Convention on the taking of evidence abroad in civil or commercial matters. Done at the Hague, March 18, 1970

States parties: Czechoslovakia, Denmark, Finland, *France, Federal Republic of Germany*, Israel, *Italy*, Luxembourg, Norway, Portugal, Sweden, Singapore, *United Kingdom, United States.*

Article 1 of this Convention states that:

> 'In civil or commercial matters, a judicial authority of a Contracting State may, in accordance with the provisions of the Contracting State, request the competent authority of another Contracting State, by means of a Letter of Request, to obtain evidence, or to obtain some other judicial act.
>
> A Letter shall not be used to obtain evidence which is not intended for use in judicial proceedings, actual or contemplated ...'

The same difficulties as outlined above, under 11.1.1, apply here regarding the definition of 'civil or commercial matters'.

The Report of the Commission at the Hague (1978) rejected the narrow interpretation of this term in the light of the liberal motives behind the Convention, and rejected the suggestion that the term should be defined according to the view of the state requested, rather than the requesting State. This Commission also urged that applications under the Convention should only be rejected when a clearly non-Civil ie. Criminal, Tax or Administrative proceeding is under way, but not when the mere possibility of a subsequent non-Civil proceeding exists.

The U.S. Hague Commission's report (1978) acceded to the proposition that evidence obtained under the Convention for use in a civil or commercial matter might later be used in a criminal proceeding. This is in contrast to the view of Viscount Dilhorne in the House of Lords during the *Westinghouse* case, where he said:

> 'But I hope that the courts of this Country will always be vigilant to prevent a misuse of the convention and will not make an order requiring evidence to be given by such persons unless it is clearly established that even if it is required for Civil proceedings, it is not also sought for criminal'.

A similar definitional problem is involved in the term 'judicial authority'. The House of Lords did not regard the American Grand Jury as such. Administrative bodies provided with investigative powers, e.g. the Securities and Exchange Commission, would probably not be regarded by U.K. Courts as judicial authorities.

Article 23 of the Convention provides the possibility for a Contracting State, at the time of signature, ratification or accession, to declare that it will not execute Letters of Request issued for the purpose of obtaining pretrial discovery of documents as known in common law countries. Declarations in these terms have been made by the governments of France and Germany and by the government of the United Kingdom which, however, added a further declaration, viz:

> 'Her Majesty's Government further declare that Her Majesty's Government understand "Letters of Request issued for the purpose of obtaining pre-trial discovery of documents" for the purposes of the foregoing Declaration as including any Letter of Request which requires a person:
>
> a) to state what documents relevant to the proceedings to which the Letter of Request relates are, or have been, in his possession, custody, or power, or
>
> b) to produce any documents other than particular documents specified in the Letter of Request as being documents appearing in the requested court, to be, or to be likely to be, in his possession, custody or power.'

Quite how far the questions asked in Letters of Request are to be cut down by such declarations is uncertain. Certainly the courts should not refuse to effect such requests on too strict a basis, for it will not always be possible for them to judge whether the evidence will be relevant and admissible.

These are but some examples of the potential difficulties involved in operating the Convention. Article 11 (witness may refuse to give evidence insofar as is under a duty or has a privilege so to do) and Article 12 (State may refuse to execute a letter of request where it considers that its sovereignty or security would be prejudiced thereby) are also potential problem areas.

### 11.1.3 OECD Recommendation concerning cooperation between member states on restrictive business practices of the organisation for economic cooperation and development (OECD)

The most recent form of this Recommendation is of September 25, 1979, replacing earlier versions of October 5, 1967 and July 3, 1973. The 1979 Recommendation provides for the notification, exchange of information and coordination of the enforcement proceedings of the OECD member countries with respect to restrictive commercial practices affecting international trade. The Recommendation also provides for consultation and conciliation procedures between member States. If a satisfactory solution is not found by consultation, the interested member States may submit the case to the Experts Committee on Commercial Restrictive Practices for conciliation.

These procedures have been used in a number of cases involving the U.S. and German governments and others.

### 11.1.4 European Convention on mutual assistance in criminal matters of April 20, 1959

As of December 31, 1979, the Convention was in force in:

Belgium, Denmark, *Federal Republic of Germany, France*, Greece, Israel, *Italy*, Lichtenstein, Luxembourg, Netherlands, Norway, Austria, Sweden, *Switzerland*, Turkey.

Although, in general, the Convention also covers administrative offence procedures, it is not applicable in procedures of administrative authorities. It is therefore of limited usefulness in antitrust matters.

In Article 1, the Convention provides that the contracting states undertake to afford each other the widest measure of mutual assistance in proceedings with respect to offences which fall under the competence of the *judicial authorities*. The mutual assistance includes the service of writs and records of judicial verdicts and the hearing of witnesses or experts. Furthermore, it pertains to the exchange of documents and other information between the competent authorities.

By special agreement, the Convention provisions do cover administrative proceedings between Switzerland and Germany.

## 11.2 BILATERAL AGREEMENTS

### 11.2.1 USA – Germany

Agreement between the Governments of the United States of America and the Federal Republic of Germany on Mutual Cooperation in the Field of Restrictive Business Practices, of June 23, 1976. (Text attached as Appendix 2). German Text published in WuW 76, p. 578.

For the basic provisions of the agreement see App. 2. It is important to mention that the exchange of confidential information is not a subject of the Agreement. Therefore, the German cartel authorities are not entitled to disclose any business or trade secrets to the U.S. antitrust authorities, as they would thereby commit a criminal offence according to paragraph 203 sub paragraph 2 of the German criminal code. Also such confidential information, which the German authorities have got from the EEC antitrust authorities according to regulation 17 cannot be disclosed to the U.S. antitrust authorities. Finally, the information which has been made available to the antitrust authorities by the other party may only be used for the purpose of antitrust procedures, but not for civil procedures, tax proceedings etc.

The U.S. – German treaty has already been applied in a number of cases since it has been in force. In 1978, *e.g.*, the treaty was the legal basis for an exchange of information in seven cases. (Annual Report of the BKartA 1978, at 44).

In a recent case, however, in which the U.S. antitrust authorities had requested information, the German antitrust authorities were unable to deliver the information requested by the U.S. authorities because of its confidentiality.

As only voluntary compliance with a request for information is covered by the provisions of the treaty, subpoenas of U.S. courts cannot be passed on by the German antitrust authorities.

It appears that the U.S. antitrust authorities have informed the BKartA of every procedure which has been directed against German enterprises in the U.S.

### 11.2.2 USA – Canada

5 Trade Reg. Rep. (CHH) 50, 112 (Nov. 3, 1969); Stevenson, *Extraterritoriality in Canadian-United States Relations*, 63 Dep't State Bull. 425 (1970).

### 11.2.3 USA – General

Several Treaties of Friendship Commerce and Navigation between the U.S. and foreign countries contain restrictive business practices consultation clauses. *See* Haight, *The Restrictive Business Practices Clause in United States Treaties: An Antitrust Tranquilizer for International Trade*, 70 Yale L.J. 240 (1960).

### 11.2.4 Germany – Japan

Negotiations are in process with Japan concerning an agreement similar to that with the U.S. Apparently, however, these negotiations are currently at a standstill, and their outcome is uncertain.

### 11.2.5 EEC – EFTA etc.

Under Reg. 17/62, Art. 10, there is detailed provision for liaison with the competent authorities of Member States in antitrust matters.

The free trade agreements between the Community and the EFTA countries (Austria, Finland, Norway, Portugal, Sweden and Switzerland) and the agreement with Israel contain similar provisions to the rules of competition of the EEC treaty. To the extent that any restrictive practice affects trade between the Community and the signatory country, each of the two contracting parties may bring the matter to the attention of the Joint Committee set up under the agreement and thereafter adopt safeguard measures. The Joint Committee should be presented with all the relevant information with a view to seeking a solution acceptable to all the contracting parties.

### 11.2.6 France

None

### 11.2.7 U.K.

None

### 11.2.8 Switzerland

None

### 11.2.9 Italy

None

### 11.2.10 Australia

None

## 11.3 SPECIAL NOTE REGARDING THE EEC

Pursuant to Article 13(1) of Regulation 17/62, the Commission has the power to request the competent authorities of the Member States to undertake the investigations which the Commission considers necessary under Article 14(1), or which it has ordered by decision pursuant to Article 14(3). Unfortunately, no guide lines have yet been established as to the way in which the Commission may exercise its powers under Article 13(1). Although this provision refers mainly to investigations to be carried out by the competent authorities in the Member State in whose territory the investigation is to be made, the powers granted to the Commission are not limited in this respect. Thus, to the extent that a Member State has been given certain powers of investigation in a non-EEC country, pursuant to a treaty or other agreement which it has concluded with that country, it is not excluded that the Commission could request the competent authorities of that Member State to exercise those powers in connection with an investigation which the Commission considers to be necessary under Article 14(1) of Regulation 17.

In such a case, it would, of course, be necessary to ascertain whether all the conditions for the exercise of the Member State's power of investigation have been met. In particular, it would be necessary to determine whether the power of investigation of the Member State could be exercised in a proceeding relating to the application of the EEC antitrust rules. Since the EEC antitrust rules are part of the internal legal system of all the EEC Member States and may be directly applied by the competent authorities and the courts of all the Member States, it may be likely that the powers of investigation of the Member State could be considered broad enough to cover an investigation directed to the application of the EEC rules.

Nevertheless, one should consider that the investigation may expose the foreign company to the fines or periodic penalty payments provided by Regulation 17/62 which may be imposed exclusively by the Commission. One should thus also consider whether the exposure to such risk is acceptable under the treaty or other agreement which gives the Member State the power of investigation.

In this context, it may be relevant whether the alleged violation of the EEC antitrust rules under investigation has an effect on competition within the Member State which the Commission has requested to carry out the investigation. First, when the practice under investigation affects competition within the Member State which has been requested to carry out the investigation, the legitimacy of such an investigation under the relevant treaty or other agreement is less likely to be considered. Second, the practice under investigation may also constitute a violation of the internal antitrust rules of the Member State and thus be subject to the imposition of fines by the competent authorities of that Member State. In such a case, the practice under investigation would already have exposed the non-EEC company to the imposition of fines. Although the investigation may result also in the imposition of fines by the Commission, the additional risk of fines is somewhat limited by what the Court states in *Wilhelm v. Bundeskartellamt* (Case 14/68, [1969] ECR 1 at 15):

'if, however, the possibility of two procedures being conducted separately were to lead to the imposition of consecutive sanctions, a general requirement of natural justice, such as that expressed at the end of the second paragraph of Article 90 of the ECSC Treaty, demands that any previous punitive decision must be taken into account in determining any sanction which is to be imposed.'

# Appendices

# 1. United States Federal Rules of Civil Procedure

RULE 37. FAILURE TO MAKE OR COOPERATE IN DISCOVERY: SANCTIONS

**(a) Motion for Order Compelling Discovery**

A party upon reasonable notice to other parties and all persons affected thereby, may apply for an order compelling discovery as follows:

*(1) Appropriate Court*

An application for an order to a party may be made to the court in which the action is pending, or, on matters relating to a deposition, to the court in the district where the deposition is being taken. An application for an order to a deponent who is not a party shall be made to the court in the district where the deposition is being taken.

*(2) Motion*

If a deponent fails to answer a question propounded or submitted under Rules 30 or 31, or a corporation or other entity fails to make a designation under Rule 30 (b) (6) or 31 (a), or a party fails to answer an interrogatory submitted under Rule 33, or if a party, in response to a request for inspection submitted under Rule 34, fails to respond that inspection will be permitted as requested or fails to permit inspection as requested, the discovering party may move for an order compelling an answer, or a designation, or an order compelling inspection in accordance with the request. When taking a deposition on oral examination, the proponent of the question may complete or adjourn the examination before he applies for an order.

If the court denies the motion in whole or in part, it may make such protective order as it would have been empowered to make on a motion made pursuant to Rule 26 (c).

*(3) Evasive or Incomplete Answer*

For purposes of this subdivision an evasive or incomplete answer is to be treated as a failure to answer.

*(4) Award of Expenses of Motion*

If the motion is granted, the court shall, after opportunity for hearing, require the party or deponent whose conduct necessitated the motion or the party or attorney advising such conduct or both of them to pay to the moving party the reasonable expenses incurred in obtaining the order, including attorney's fees, unless the court finds that the opposition to the motion was substantially justified or that other circumstances make an award of expenses unjust.

If the motion is denied, the court shall, after opportunity for hearing, require the moving party or the attorney advising the motion or both of them to pay to the party or deponent who opposed the motion the reasonable expenses incurred in opposing the motion, including attorney's fees, unless the court finds that the making of the motion was substantially justified or that other circumstances make an award of expenses unjust.

If the motion is granted in part and denied in part, the court may apportion the reasonable expenses incurred in relation to the motion among the parties and persons in a just manner.

**(b) Failure to Comply with Order**

*(1) Sanctions by Court in District Where Deposition is Taken*

If a deponent fails to be sworn or to answer a question after being directed to do so by the court in the district in which the deposition is being taken, the failure may be considered as a contempt of that court.

*(2) Sanctions by Court in which Action is Pending*

If a party or an officer, director or managing agent of a party or a person designated under Rule 30 (b) (6) or 31 (a) to testify on behalf of a party fails to obey an order to provide or permit discovery, including an order made under subdivision (a) of this rule or Rule 35, or if a party fails to obey an order entered under Rule 26 (f), the court in which the action is pending may make such orders in regard to the failure as are just, and among others the following:

(A) An order that the matters regarding which the order was made or any other designated facts shall be taken to be established for the purposes of the action in accordance with the claim of the party obtaining the order;

(B) An order refusing to allow the disobedient party to support or oppose designated claims or defences, or prohibiting him from introducing designated matters in evidence;

(C) An order striking out pleadings or parts thereof, or staying further proceedings until the order is obeyed, or dismissing the action or proceeding or any part thereof, or rendering a judgment by default against the disobedient party;

(D) In lieu of any of the foregoing orders or in addition thereto, an order treating as contempt of court the failure to obey any orders except an order to submit to a physical or mental examination;

(E) Where a party has failed to comply with an order under Rule 35 (a) requiring him to produce another for examination, such orders as are listed in paragraphs (A), (B) and (C) of this subdivision, unless the party failing to comply shows that he is unable to produce such person for examination.

In lieu of any of the foregoing orders or in addition thereto, the court shall require the party failing to obey the order or the attorney advising him or both to pay the reasonable expenses, including attorney's fees, caused by the failure, unless the court finds that the failure was substantially justified or that other circumstances make an award of expenses unjust.

**(c) Expenses on Failure to Admit**

If a party fails to admit the genuineness of any document or the truth of any matter as requested under Rule 36, and if the party requesting the admissions thereafter proves the genuineness of the document or the truth of the matter, he may apply to the court for an order requiring the other party to pay him the reasonable expenses incurred in making the proof, including reasonable attorney's fees. The court shall make the order unless it finds that (1) the request was held objectionable pursuant to Rule 36 (a), or (2) the admission sought was of no substantial importance, or (3) the party failing to admit had reasonable ground to believe that he might prevail on the matter, or (4) there was other good reason for the failure to admit.

**(d) Failure of Party to Attend at Own Deposition or Serve Answers to Interrogatories or Respond to Request for Inspection**

If a party or an officer, director, or managing agent of a party or a person designated under Rule 30 (b) (6) or 31 (a) to testify on behalf of a party fails (1) to appear before the officer who is to take his deposition, after being served with a proper notice or (2) to serve answers or objections to interrogatories submitted under Rule 33, after proper service of the interrogatories, or (3) to serve a written response to a request for inspection submitted under Rule 34, after proper service of the request, the court in which the action is pending on motion may make such orders in regard to the failure as are just, and among others it may take any action authorised under paragraphs (A), (B) and (C) of subdivision (b) (2) of this rule. In lieu of any order or in addition thereto, the court shall require the party failing to act or the attorney advising him or both to pay the reasonable expenses, including attorney's fees, caused by the failure, unless the court finds that the failure was substantially justified or that other circumstances make an award of expenses unjust.

The failure to act described in this subdivision may not be excused on the ground that the discovery sought is objectionable unless the party failing to act has applied for a protective order as provided by Rule 26 (c).

**(f) Expenses Against United States**

Except to the extent permitted by statute, expenses and fees may not be awarded against the United States under this rule.

**(g) Failure to Participate in the Framing of a Discovery Plan**

If a party or his attorney fails to participate in good faith in the framing of a discovery plan by agreement as is required by Rule 26 (f), the court may, after opportunity for hearing, require such party or his attorney to pay to any other party the reasonable expenses, including attorney's fees, caused by the failure.

As amended Dec. 29, 1948, eff. Oct. 20, 1949; March 30, 1970, eff. Juli 1, 1970; April 29, 1980, eff. Aug. 1, 1980.

# 2. Relevant Provisions of the U.S./German Cooperation Agreement (5 Trade Reg. Rep. (CHH) 50,283)

**Article 2**

(1) Each party agrees that its antitrust authorities will cooperate and render assistance to the antitrust authorities of the other party, to the extent set forth in this Agreement, in connection with:

(a) antitrust investigations or proceedings,

(b) studies related to competition policy and possible changes in antitrust laws, and

(c) activities related to the restrictive business practice work of international organisations of which both parties are members.

(2) Each party agrees that it will provide the other party with any significant information which comes to the attention of its antitrust authorities and which involves restrictive business practices which, regardless or origin, have a substantial effect on the domestic or international trade of such other party.

(3) Each party agrees that, upon request of the other party, its antitrust authorities will obtain for and furnish such other party with such information as such other party may request in connection with a matter referred to in Article 2, paragraph 1, and will otherwise provide advice and assistance in connection therewith. Such advice and assistance shall include, but not necessarily be limited to, the exchange of information and a summary of experience relating to particular practices where either of the antitrust authorities of the requested party has dealt with or has information relating to a practice involved in the request. Such assistance shall also include the attendance of public officials of the requested party to give information, views or testimony in regard to any antitrust investigation or proceeding, legislation or policy, and the transmittal or the making available of documents and legal briefs and pleadings of the antitrust authorities of the requested party (or duly authenticated or certified copies thereof).

(4) An antitrust authority of a party, in seeking to obtain information or interviews on a voluntary basis from a person or enterprise within the jurisdiction of the other party, may request such other party to transmit a communication seeking such information or interviews to such person or communication and, if so requested, will (if such is the case) notify such person or enterprise that the requested party has no objection to voluntary compliance with the request.

(5) Each party agrees that, upon the request of an antitrust authority of the other party, its antitrust authorities will consult with the requesting party concerning possible coordination of concurrent antitrust investigations or proceedings in the two countries which are related or affect each other.

**Article 3**

(1) Either party may decline, in whole or in part, to render assistance under Article 2 of this Agreement, or may comply with any request for such assistance subject to such terms and conditions as the complying party may establish, if such party determines that: –

(a) compliance would be prohibited by legal protections of confidentiality or by other domestic law of the complying party; or

(b) compliance would be inconsistent with its security, public policy or other important national interests;

(c) the requesting party is unable or unwilling to comply with terms or conditions established by the complying party, including conditions designed to protect the confidentiality of information requested; or

(d) the requesting party would not be obligated to comply with such request, by reason of any grounds set forth in items (a), (b) or (c) above, if such request had been made by the requested party.

(2) Neither party shall be obligated to employ compulsory powers in order to obtain information for, or otherwise provide advice and assistance to, the other party pursuant to this Agreement.

(3) Neither party shall be obligated to undertake efforts in connection with this Agreement which are likely to require such substantial utilisation of personnel or resources as to burden unreasonably its own enforcement duties.

# 3. Protection of Trading Interests Act 1980 - U.K.

1980 CHAPTER II

An Act to provide protection from requirements, prohibitions and judgments imposed or given under the laws of countries outside the United Kingdom and affecting the trading or other interests of persons in the United Kingdom [20th March 1980].

Be it enacted by the Queen's most Excellent Majesty, by and with the advice and consent of the Lords Spiritual and Temporal, and Commons, in this present Parliament assembled, and by the authority of the same, as follows:

1. (1) If it appears to the Secretary of State –

(a) that measures have been or are proposed to be taken by or under the law of any overseas country for regulating or controlling international trade; and

(b) that those measures, insofar as they apply or would apply to things done or to be done outside the territorial jurisdiction of that country by persons carrying on business in the United Kingdom, are damaging or threaten to damage the trading interests of the United Kingdom

the Secretary of State may by order direct that this section shall apply to those measures either generally or in their application to such cases as may be specified in the order.

(2) The Secretary of State may by order make provision for requiring, or enabling the Secretary of State to require, a person in the United Kingdom who carries on business there to give notice to the Secretary of State of any requirement or prohibition imposed or threatened to be imposed on that person pursuant to any measures insofar as this section applies to them by virtue of an order under subsection (1) above

(3) The Secretary of State may give to any person in the United Kingdom who carries on business there such directions for prohibiting compliance with any such requirement or prohibition as aforesaid as he considers appropriate for avoiding damage to the trading interests of the United Kingdom.

(4) The power of the Secretary of State to make orders under subsection (1) or (2) above shall be exercisable by statutory instrument subject to annulment in pursuance of a resolution of either House of Parliament.

(5) Directions under subsection (3) above may be either general or special and may prohibit compliance with any requirement or prohibition either absolutely or in such cases or subject to such conditions as to consent or otherwise as may be specified in the directions; and general directions under that subsection shall be published in such manner as appears to the Secretary of State to be appropriate.

(6) In this section 'trade' includes any activity carried on in the course of a business of any description and 'trading interests' shall be construed accordingly.

2. (1) If it appears to the Secretary of State –

(a) that a requirement has been or may be imposed on a person or persons in the United Kingdom to produce to any court, tribunal or authority of an overseas country any commercial document which is not within the territorial jurisdiction of that country or to furnish any commercial information to any court, tribunal or authority; or

(b) that any such authority has imposed or may impose a requirement on a person or persons in the United Kingdom to publish any such document or information

the Secretary of State may, if it appears to him that the requirement is inadmissible by virtue of subsection (2) or (3) below, give directions for prohibiting compliance with the requirement.

(2) A requirement such as is mentioned in subsection (1) (a) or (b) above is inadmissible –

(a) if it infringes the jurisdiction of the United Kingdom or is otherwise prejudicial to the sovereignty of the United Kingdom; or

(b) if compliance with the requirement would be prejudical to the security of the United Kingdom or to the relations of the government of the United Kingdom with the government of any other country.

(3) A requirement such as is mentioned in subsection (1) (a) above is also inadmissible –

(a) if it is made otherwise than for the purposes of civil or criminal proceedings which have been instituted in the overseas country; or

(b) if it requires a person to state what documents relevant to any such proceedings are or have been in his possession, custody or power or to produce for the purposes of any such proceedings any document other than particular documents specified in the requirement.

(4) Directions under subsection (1) above may be either general or special and may prohibit compliance with any requirement either absolutely or in such cases or subject to such conditions as to consent or otherwise as may be specified in the directions; and general directions under that subsection shall be published in such manner as appears to the Secretary of State to be appropriate.

(5) For the purposes of this section the making of a request or demand shall be treated as the imposition of a requirement if it is made in circumstances in which a requirement to the same effect could be or could have been imposed; and

(a) any request or demand for the supply of a document or information which, pursuant to the requirement of any court, tribunal or authority of an overseas country, is addressed to a person in the United Kingdom; or

(b) any requirement imposed by such a court, tribunal or authority to produce or furnish any document or information to a person specified in the requirement

shall be treated as a requirement to produce or furnish that document or information to that court, tribunal or authority.

(6) In this section 'commercial document' and 'commercial information' means respectively a document or information relating to a business of any description and 'document' includes any record or device by means of which material is recorded or stored.

3. (1) Subject to subsection (2) below, any person who without reasonable excuse fails to comply with any requirement imposed under subsection (2) of section 1 above or knowingly contravenes any directions given under subsection (3) of that section or section 2 (1) above shall be guilty of an offence and liable –

(a) on conviction on indictment to a fine;

(b) on summary conviction, to a fine not exceeding the statutory minimum.

(2) A person who is neither a citizen of the United Kingdom and Colonies nor a body corporate incorporated in the United Kingdom shall not be guilty of an offence under subsection (1) above by reason of anything done or omitted outside the United Kingdom in contravention of directions under section 1 (3) or 2 (1) above.

(3) No proceedings for an offence under subsection (a) above shall be instituted in England, Wales or Northern Ireland except by the Secretary of State or with the consent of the Attorney General or, as the case may be, the Attorney General for Northern Ireland.

(4) Proceedings against any person for an offence under this section may be taken before the appropriate court in the United Kingdom having jurisdiction in the place where that person is for the time being.

, (5) In subsection (1) above 'the statutory maximum' means –

(a) in England and Wales and Northern Ireland, the prescribed sum within the meaning of section 28 of the Criminal Law Act 1977 (at the passing of this Act £1,000);

(b) in Scotland, the prescribed sum within the meaning of section 289B of the Criminal Procedure (Scotland) Act 1975 (at the passing of this Act £1,000); and for the purposes of the application of this subsection in Northern Ireland the provisions of the said Act of 1977 relating to the sum mentioned in paragraph (a) shall extend to Northern Ireland.

4. A court in the United Kingdom shall not make an order under section 2 of the Evidence (Proceedings in Other Jurisdictions) Act 1975 for giving effect to a request issued by or on behalf of a court or tribunal of an overseas country if it is shown that the request infringes the jurisdiction of the United Kingdom or is otherwise prejudicial to the sovereignty of the United Kingdom; and a certificate signed by or on behalf of the Secretary of State to the effect that it infringes that jurisdiction or is so prejudicial shall be conclusive evidence of that fact.

5. (1) A judgment to which this section applies shall not be registered under Part II of the Administration of Justice Act 1920 or Part I of the Foreign Judgments (Reciprocal Enforcement) Act 1933 and no court in the United Kingdom shall entertain proceedings at common law for the recovery of any sum payable under such a judgment.

(2) This section applies to any judgment given by a court of an overseas country, being –

(a) a judgment for multiple damages within the meaning of subsection (3) below;

(b) a judgment based on a provision or rule of law specified or described in an order under subsection (4) below and given after the coming into force of the order; or

(c) a judgment on a claim for contribution in respect of damages awarded by a judgment falling within paragraph (a) or (b) above

(3) In subsection (2) (a) above judgment for multiple damages means a judgment for an amount arrived at by doubling, trebling or otherwise multiplying a sum assessed as compensation for the loss or damage sustained by the person in whose favour the judgment is given.

(4) The Secretary of State may for the purposes of subsection (2) (b) above make an order in respect of any provision or rule of law which appears to him to be concerned with the prohibition or regulation of agreements, arrangements or practices designed to restrain, distort or restrict competition in the carrying on of business of any description or to be otherwise concerned with the promotion of such competition as aforesaid.

(5) The power of the Secretary of State to make orders under subsection (4) above shall be exercisable by statutory instrument subject to annulment in pursuance of a resolution of either House of Parliament.

(6) Subsection (2) (a) above applies to a judgment given before the date of the passing of this Act as well as to a judgment given on or after that date but this section does not affect any judgment which has been registered before that date under the provisions mentioned in subsection (1) above or in respect of which such proceedings as are there mentioned have been finally determined before that date.

6. (1) This section applies where a court of an overseas country has given a judgment for multiple damages within the meaning of section 5 (3) above against –

(a) a citizen of the United Kingdom or Colonies; or

(b) a body corporate incorporated in the United Kingdom or in a territory outside the United Kingdom for whose international relations Her Majesty's Government in the United Kingdom are responsible; or

(c) A person carrying on business in the United Kingdom.

(in this section referred to as a 'qualifying defendant') and an amount on account of the damages has been paid by the qualifying defendant either to the party in whose favour the judgment was given or to another party who is entitled as against the qualifying defendant to contribution in respect of the damages.

(2) Subject to subsections (3) and (4) below, the qualifying defendant shall be entitled to recover from the party in whose favour the judgment was given so much of the amount referred to in subsection (1) above as exceeds the part attributable to compensation; and that part shall be taken to be such part of the amount as bears to the whole of it the same proportion as the sum assessed by the court that gave the judgment as compensation for the loss or damage sustained by that party bears to the whole of the damages awarded to that party.

(3) Subsection (2) above does not apply where the qualifying defendant is an individual who was ordinarily resident in the overseas country at the time when the proceedings in which the judgment was given were instituted or a body corporate which had its principal place of business there at that time.

(4) Subsection (2) above does not apply where the qualifying defendant carried on business in the overseas country and the proceedings in which the judgment was given were concerned with activities exclusively carried on in that country.

(5) A court in the United Kingdom may entertain proceedings on a claim under this section notwithstanding that the person against whom the proceedings are brought is not within the jurisdiction of the court.

(6) The reference in subsection (1) above to an amount paid by the qualifying defendant includes a reference to an amount obtained by execution against his property or

against the property of a company which (directly or indirectly) is wholly owned by him; and references in that subsection and subsection (2) above to the party in whose favour the judgment was given or to a party entitled to contribution include references to any person in whom the rights of any such party have become vested by succession or assignment or otherwise.

(7) This section shall, with the necessary modifications, apply also in relation to any order which is made by a tribunal or authority of an overseas country and would if that tribunal or authority were a court, be a judgment for multiple damages within the meaning of section 5 (3) above.

(8) This section does not apply to any judgment given or order made before the passing of this Act.

7. (1) If it appears to Her Majesty that the law of an overseas country provides or will provide for the enforcement in that country of judgments given under section 6 above, Her Majesty may by Order in Council provide for the enforcement in the United Kingdom of judgments given under any provision of the law of that country corresponding to that section.

(2) An Order under this section may apply, with or without modification, any of the provisions of the Foreign Judgments (Reciprocal Enforcement) Act 1933.

8. (1) This Act may be cited as the Protection of Trading Interests Act 1980.

(2) In this Act 'overseas country' means any country or territory outside the United Kingdom other than one for whose international relations Her Majesty's Government in the United Kingdom are responsible.

(3) References in this Act to the law or a court, tribunal or authority of an overseas country include, in the case of a federal state, references to the law or a court, tribunal or authority of any constituent part of that country.

(4) References in this Act to a claim for, or to entitlement to, contribution are references to a claim or entitlement based on an enactment or rule of law.

(5) The Shipping Contracts and Commercial Documents Act 1964 (which is superseded by this Act) is hereby repealed, together with paragraph 18 of Schedule 2 and paragraph 24 of Schedule 3 to the Criminal Law Act 1977 (which contain amendments of that Act).

(6) Subsection (5) above shall not affect the operation of the said Act of 1964 in relation to any directions given under that Act before the passing of this Act.

(7) This Act extends to Northern Ireland.

(8) Her Majesty may by Order in Council direct that this Act shall extend with such exceptions, adaptations and modifications, if any, as may be specified in the Order to any territory outside the United Kingdom, being a territory for the international relations of which Her Majesty's Government in the United Kingdom are responsible.

# 4. Italy - Shipping Documents Act 1980 (Unofficial Translation)

THE ACT

Act 488 of 24 July 1980 to prohibit Italian citizens from supplying to foreign authorities documents and information concerning maritime activity.

The Chamber of Deputies and the Senate of the Republic have approved, and the President of the Republic hereby promulgates, the following statute:

**Section 1**

[1] Shipowners, their representatives or heads of Italian shipping companies must transmit to the Ministry of Merchant Shipping, within thirty days of receipt thereof, a copy of any orders issued by foreign authorities to supply information or to send documents relating to the administrative or financial management of the enterprise or to commercial agreements about maritime charters and services.

[2] Whoever fails to comply with the preceding subsection shall be punished with an administrative fine of between 100,000 lire and one million lire. Sections 3 to 9 of Act 706 of 24 December 1975, as amended, shall apply.

**Section 2**

[1] Whoever supplies the information or sends the documents referred to in the first subsection of section 1 to foreign authorities shall, unless that action has been authorised by the competent department of state, be punished by imprisonment not exceeding two months or by a fine not exceeding 5 million lire or by both such imprisonment and such fine.

[2] The provisions of the preceding sub-section shall apply even if the act is committed abroad.

# 5. Canadian Bill C-41 July 11, 1980

An Act to authorise the making of orders relating to the production of records and the giving of information for the purposes of proceedings in foreign tribunals and in respect of the recognition and enforcement in Canada of certain foreign judgments obtained in antitrust proceedings.

Her Majesty, by and with the advice and consent of the Senate and House of Commons of Canada, enacts as follows:

**Short title**

1. This Act may be cited as the FOREIGN PROCEEDINGS AND JUDGMENTS ACT.

**Interpretation**

2. In this Act,

'antitrust law' means a law of a foreign jurisdiction of a kind commonly known as an antitrust law and includes a law having as a purpose the preservation of competition between business enterprises or the prevention or repression of monopolies or restrictive practices in trade or commerce;

'foreign tribunal' means a tribunal of a country other than Canada or of a part of such a country;

'judgment' includes a decree or order;

'record' includes any correspondence, memorandum, book, plan, map, drawing, diagram, pictorial or graphic work, photograph, film, microform, sound recording, videotape, machine readable record, and any other documentary material, regardless of physical form or characteristics, and any copy or portion thereof;

'tribunal' includes a court, body, authority or person having authority to take or receive information, whether on its or his behalf or on behalf of any other court, body, authority or person.

**Disclosure of records to foreign tribunals**

*Orders of the Attorney General*

3. (1) Where, in the opinion of the Attorney General of Canada, a foreign tribunal is exercising or is proposing or likely to exercise jurisdiction or powers of a kind or in a manner that will adversely affect significant Canadian interests in relation to international trade or commerce involving a business carried out in whole or in part in Canada, he may by order prohibit or restrict

(a) the production before or the disclosure or identification to, or for the purposes of, a foreign tribunal of records that, at any time while the order is in force, are in Canada or are in the possession or under the control of a Canadian citizen or a person resident in Canada;

(b) the doing of any act in Canada, in relation to records that at any time while the order is in force are in Canada or are in the possession or under the control of a Canadian citizen or a person resident in Canada, that will, or is likely to, result in the records, or information as to the contents of the records or from which the records might be identified, being produced or disclosed or identified to, or for the purposes of, a foreign tribunal; and

(c) the giving by a person, at a time when he is a Canadian citizen or a resident of Canada, of information before a foreign tribunal in relation to, or in relation to the contents or identification of, records that, at any time while the order is in force, are or were in Canada.

(2) Where production before or disclosure or identification to, or for the purposes of, a foreign tribunal of a record and the giving by a person of information before a foreign tribunal in relation to, or in relation to the contents or identification of, a record is prohibited or restricted by an order under subsection (1), a tribunal in Canada shall not, for the purposes of proceedings before the foreign tribunal,

(a) where the order is in the nature of a prohibition, receive the record or information in relation to, or in relation to the contents or identification of, the record; or

(b) where the order is in the nature of a restriction, receive the record or information in relation to, or in relation to the contents or identification of, the record if, as a result of so doing, the order may be contravened.

(3) An order under this section may

(a) be directed to a particular person or to a class of persons;

(b) relate to a particular foreign tribunal or to a class of foreign tribunals; and

(c) relate to a particular record or to a class of records.

4. (1) An order under section 3

(a) may be served on a person, other than a corporation, to whom it is directed by delivering it personally to him or, if that person cannot conveniently be found, by leaving it for him at his last or usual place of residence with some person found therein who appears to be at least sixteen years of age; or

(b) may be served on a corporation to which it is directed by delivering it personally to the manager, secretary or other executive officer of the corporation or of a branch thereof.

(2) Where, on an application by or on behalf of the Attorney General of Canada, a superior court is satisfied that an order under section 3 that is directed to a class of persons cannot reasonably be served in the manner described in paragraph (1) (a) or (b) on all or any of the persons included in the class, it may, by order, authorise service of the order on those persons in such other manner as it considers appropriate.

(3) An order varying or revoking an order under section 3 may be served on the person to whom it is directed in any manner in which the order could have been served on that person.

*Seizure of records*

5. Where, on an application by or on behalf of the Attorney General of Canada, a superior court is satisfied that an order under section 3 may not be complied with in relation to some or all of the records in Canada to which it relates, the court may issue a warrant authorising a person named therein or a peace officer to seize those records and to deliver them to the court or a person designated by the court for safekeeping while the order under section 3 remains in force, on such terms as to access to the records or return of all or any of the records, as are fixed by the court having regard to the object to which the order under section 3 is directed.

*Offences*

6. (1) Every one who contravenes an order under section 3 that is directed to him and that has been served on him in accordance with section 4

(a) is guilty of an indictable offence and is liable to a fine of ten thousand dollars or to imprisonment for five years or to both or

(b) is guilty of an offence punishable on summary conviction and is liable to a fine of five thousand dollars or to imprisonment for two years or both.

(2) A contravention of an order under paragraph 3 (1) (a) or (c) that would be punishable as an offence under subsection (1) if committed in Canada is

(a) if committed outside Canada by Canadian citizen or a person resident in Canada, in the case of an order under paragraph 3 (1) (a), and

(b) if committed outside Canada by any person, in the case of an order under paragraph 3 (a) (c)

an offence under this Act that may be tried and punished in Canada, and proceedings in respect of such an offence may be instituted, tried and determined in any place in Canada.

(3) No proceedings with respect to an offence under this Act may be instituted without the consent of the Attorney General of Canada.

**Recognition and enforcements of foreign judgments**

*Orders of the Attorney General*

7. (1) Where a foreign tribunal has, whether before or after the coming into force of this Act, given a judgment in proceedings instituted under an antitrust law and, in the opinion of the Attorney General of Canada, the recognition or enforcement of the judgment in Canada will adversely affect significant Canadian interests in relation to international trade or commerce involving a business carried on in whole or in part in Canada, he may

(a) by order declare that the judgment shall not be recognised or enforceable in any manner in Canada; and

(b) in the case of a judgment for a specified amount of money by order declare that for the purposes of the recognition and enforcement of the judgment in Canada the amount of the judgment shall be deemed to be reduced to such amount as is specified in the order.

(2) Every order made by the Attorney General of Canada under subsection (1) shall be published in the Canada Gazette and each such order comes into force on the later of the day it is so published and a day specified in the order as the day on which it is to come into force.

(3) While an order made by the Attorney General of Canada under subsection (1) is in force:

(a) in the case of an order under paragraph (1) (a), the judgment to which it relates shall not be recognised and is not enforceable in Canada; and

(b) in the case of an order under paragraph (1) (b), the judgment to which it relates may, if enforceable apart from this Act, be recognised and enforced in Canada as if the amount specified in the order were substituted for the amount of the judgment, and not otherwise.

*Recovery of Damages*

8. (1) Where a judgment in respect of which an order has been made under section 7 has been given against a party who is a Canadian citizen, a corporation incorporated by or under a law of Canada or a province or a person carrying on business in Canada, that party may, in Canada, sue for and recover from a person in whose favour the judgment is given

(a) in the case of an order under paragraph (7) (1) (a), any amount paid to that person by that party under the judgment; and

(b) in the case of an order under paragraph (7) (1) (b), any amount paid to that person by that party under the judgment that is in excess of the amount to which the judgment is deemed to be reduced.

(2) Subsection (1) does not apply where the party referred to in that subsection

(a) is an individual who was ordinarily resident in the country in which the judgment is given at the time when the proceeding in which the judgment is given was instituted;

(b) is a corporation that had its principal place of business in the country in which the judgment is given at the time referred to in paragraph (a); or

(c) carried on business in the country in which the judgment is given through a branch or establishment in that country and the proceeding in which the judgment is given was concerned with activities exclusively carried on in that country through that branch or establishment.

(3) A court that renders judgment in favour of a party pursuant to subsection (1) may, in addition to any other means of enforcing judgment available to the court, order the seizure and sale of shares of any corporation incorporated by or under a law of Canada or a province in which the person against whom the judgment is rendered has a direct or indirect beneficial interest, whether the share certificates are located inside or outside Canada.

**Procedure for revoking orders**

9. (1) An Order under section 3 or 7 shall be laid before Parliament not later than the fifteenth sitting day of Parliament after it is made.

(2) Where, before the twentieth sitting day of Parliament after an order under section 3 or 7 has been laid before Parliament, a motion for the consideration of either House, to the effect that the order be revoked, signed by not less than fifty members of the House of Commons in the case of a motion for the consideration of that House and by not less than twenty members of the Senate in the case of a motion for the consideration of the Senate, is filed with the Speaker of the appropriate House, that House shall, not later than the sixth sitting day of that House following the filing of the motion, take up and consider the motion unless a motion to the like effect has earlier been taken up and considered in the other House.

(3) A motion taken up and considered in accordance with subsection (2) shall be debated without interruption for not more than three hours and, on the conclusion of such debate or at the expiry of the third such hour, the Speaker of the House of Commons or the Senate, as the case may be, shall forthwith, without further debate or amendment, put every question necessary for the disposal of the motion.

(4) If a motion taken up and considered in accordance with subsection (2) is adopted, with or without amendments, a message shall be sent from the House of Parliament adopting the motion informing the other House that the motion has been so adopted and requesting that the motion be concurred in by that other House.

(5) Within the first fifteen days next after receipt by it of a request pursuant to subsection (4) that the House of Parliament receiving the request is sitting, that House shall take up and consider the motion that is the subject of the request and all questions in connection therewith shall be debated without interruption for not more than three hours and, on the conclusion of such debate or at the expiry of the third such hour, the Speaker of that House shall forthwith, without further debate or amendment, put every question necessary to determine whether or not the motion in question is concurred in.

(6) Where a motion taken up and considered in accordance with this section is adopted by the House of Parliament in which it was introduced and is concurred in by the other House, the order to which the motion relates shall stand revoked but without prejudice to the prior operation thereof.

(7) For the purposes of subsections (1) and (2), 'sitting day of Parliament' means a day on which either House of Parliament sits.

10. When each House of Parliament enacts rules whereby any regulations made subject to negative resolution of Parliament within the meaning of section 28.1 of the Interpretation Act may be made the subject of a resolution of both Houses of Parliament introduced and passed in accordance with the rules of those Houses, section 9 of this Act is thereupon repealed and an order made thereafter under section 3 or 7 is an order made subject to negative resolution of Parliament within the meaning of section 28.1 of the Interpretation Act.

**Coming into force and repeal**

11. (1) This Act shall come into force on a day to be fixed by proclamation.

(2) The Uranium Information Security Regulations, Consolidated Regulations of Canada, c. 366, are repealed on the day this Act comes into force.

# 6. Domestic Effects within the Meaning of Section 98 (2) of the Act against Restraints of Competition in the Case of Mergers

*(Unofficial Translation of the Unofficial Guidelines of the German Federal Cartel Office to the Domestic Impact of Mergers)*

For an interpretation of the term 'domestic effect' within the meaning of Section 98 (2) the protective purpose of the relevant provision of the Act to be applied in each case must be considered (Federal Supreme Court decision of July 12, 1973, WuW/E 'Ölfeldrohre').

The purpose of Sections 23 et seq. is to cover concentration because it may impair competition. The term 'restraints of competition' in Section 98 (2) sums up all restraints of competition regulated in the relevant provisions of the Act. With regard to Sections 23 et seq. the restraint of competition within the meaning of Section 98 (2) is the merger process as such. It is irrelevant whether the intensity of domestic competition is actually reduced by a merger.

A. Domestic effects within the meaning of Section 98 (2) are, therefore, present *whenever* a merger is completed *within the Federal Republic*[1] (e.g. acquisition of the assets or the shares of a domestic enterprise, formation of a joint venture within the Federal Republic – even where the acquirers or the founders are foreign enterprises). As regards the domestic subsidiaries of the participating enterprises, a merger effected abroad is held to be a merger completed in the Federal Republic (Section 23 (3) sentence 4 of the ARC).

B. *Mergers completed abroad* have domestic effects if the merger affects the structural conditions for domestic competition and if the domestic enterprises (incl. subsidiaries and other affiliated companies) are a party to the merger.

1. As regards mergers effected abroad *between two directly participating enterprises only* (all merger situations except for the formation of joint ventures – e.g. acquisition of the assets or the shares of a foreign enterprise by a domestic enterprise –)

a) there are domestic effects, if both enterprises were already operating in the Federal Republic before the merger either directly or through subsidiaries, branches or importers;

b) there may be domestic effects, if only one of the enterprises was operating in the Federal Republic before the merger but if, for instance,

aa) after the merger a foreign party to the merger is likely to deliver goods to the Federal Republic due to production links with the domestic party (preceding or subsequent production stages) or of links relating to the range of products. Whether such future deliveries to the Federal Republic are likely usually depends on whether goods of the same or a similar kind are already covered by trade between the countries involved and whether there are no technical and administrative trade barriers to such deliveries;

bb) the know-how of a domestic enterprise is perceptibly enhanced or industrial property rights accrue to it as a result of the merger.

2. As regards the *formation of joint ventures* abroad, the domestic effect primarily depends on the product and geographical markets on which the joint venture operates. The question of when a joint venture's activities have domestic effects is determined on the principles set out under B.1.; in this connection the production links and/or links affecting the range of products have to be judged by the relationship between the joint venture and the domestic party.

Furthermore, the formation of a joint venture abroad may also have domestic effects, if

a) a foreign enterprise participating in the joint venture was already operating in the joint venture's field of activity within the Federal Republic before the merger or if it can be reasonably expected to enter the domestic market without the merger (cf. B.1. aa);

1. Including West Berlin

b) the domestic party to the joint venture thereby obtains additional production capacity which perceptibly alters its capacity available for domestic supply (substitution of domestic production destined for exportation by production abroad). In general, it is a prerequisite for a change in capacity being perceptible that the domestic party already enjoyed a strong market position before the merger.

# 7. Pronouncement No. 58/80 concerning the Administrative Rules of the Federal Cartel Office in respect of the export cartel notification procedure dated 8 July 1980

*(Unofficial Translation)*

I

Since the coming into force of the Fourth Act to Amend the Act Against Restraints of Competition (ARC) of 26 April 1980 – Bundesgesetzblatt (Legal Gazette) I p. 458 – the ARC has been applicable to export cartels within the meaning of Section 6 (1) of the ARC, irrespective of whether they have effect in the domestic market or markets (Section 98 (2) sentence 2 of the ARC), provided only that enterprises located in the area of application of the Act are involved. To take effect, these cartels must be notified to the Federal Cartel Office pursuant to Sections 9 (2) sentence 1, 44 (1) No. 1 lit. a of the ARC. Cartel agreements or decisions or amendments or additions thereto are of no effect pursuant to Section 1 of the ARC if they are not notified. Their implementation constitutes an administrative offence under Section 38 (1) No. 1 of the ARC punishable by a fine.

II

Export cartels take effect by notifying the cartel agreement or decision pursuant to Section 9 (2) sentence 1 of the ARC only, if the conditions set out in Section 6 (1) of the ARC are met:

– The cartel must serve to protect and to promote exports. This condition is met if the cartel is intended to strengthen the competitive position of the domestic member firms vis-à-vis their foreign competitors.

– The cartel must be limited to regulating competition outside the area of application of the ARC. Unless authorised pursuant to Section 6 (2) of the ARC, export cartels are of no effect under Section 1 of the ARC, if the cartel agreement or decision, the additional agreements or implementing decisions also provide for restrictions in respect of the trade in goods or commercial services in the area of application of the ARC.

Section 6 (1) of the ARC is applicable regardless of whether the export cartel is made up by domestic enterprises only or also by foreign enterprises.

III

Export cartels within the meaning of Section 6 (1) of the ARC are not entered in the Cartel Register nor published in the Federal Gazette.

When notifying an export cartel to the Federal Cartel Office the following particulars have to be furnished:

1. firm name or other designation and location of establishment of all the participating domestic and foreign enterprises;
2. legal form and address of the cartel;
3. name and address of the appointed representative (Section 36 of the ARC) or other agent of the cartel; in the case of legal persons, names and addresses of the legal representatives of the cartel;
4. all the arrangements made by the cartel members (agreements and decisions including additional clauses and annexes, if any) in the complete original text and, if written in a foreign language, a German translation that has been certified or made by a certified or sworn interpreter or translator (Section 23 of the Administrative Procedures Act).

Changes and additions to Nos. 1 and 4 above as well as the accession of domestic or foreign enterprises also have to be notified to the Federal Cartel Office to take effect.

Moreover, the Federal Cartel Office should be notified of changes in Nos. 2 and 3, the withdrawal of cartel members and the termination or cancellation of the agreements and decisions.

It is expedient to point out already in the application how the agreement or decision serves to protect and to promote exports, having regard to the competitive situation in the export markets.

**IV**

For existing agreements and decisions within the meaning of Section 6 (1) of the ARC the Federal Cartel Office sets a notification period ending on 31 December 1980.

The above administrative rules replace the paragraphs referring to export cartels of the Administrative Rules contained in Pronouncement No. 39/73 of 23 August 1973 (Bundesanzeiger (Federal Gazette) No. 167 of 6 September 1973).

Berlin, 8 July 1980
G 2 – 122000 – 3/78

The President of the
Federal Cartel Office
Prof. Kartte

# 8. A Factual Summary of the Westinghouse Uranium Litigation

1. After the war, the United States, which has been both the largest consumer and the largest producer of uranium, encouraged in the free world the development of uranium production.

2. Then, in 1964, the United States enacted legislation and regulations which protected the U.S. producers by barring U.S. enrichment services to foreign uranium. This had the effect of banning the use of foreign uranium in U.S. domestic reactors, which represented a large portion of the available market.

3. The foreign governments whose industries were affected – Canada, Australia, South Africa and France – became very concerned over the plight caused for their industries.

4. Thereafter, apparently with the encouragement of at least some of these governments, there were meetings among the non-U.S. producer firms in Johannesburg and elsewhere. The purpose of these meetings – as has since been described in a brief filed by the Canadian Government – was to 'allocate the meager non-U.S. demand among the non-U.S. producers, and to stabilise prices for a transitional period.'

5. Uranium prices did rise significantly in the early 1970's, whether because of the alleged cartel or for other reasons. Moreover, certain middlemen purchasers of uranium, such as Westinghouse Electric Corporation, felt that they were being boycotted by the producers and unable to obtain uranium at reasonable prices.

6. Westinghouse, in the meantime, had contracted to sell millions of tons of uranium at low prices to various U.S. utilities. When Westinghouse defaulted because of the greatly increased cost of uranium, the utilities sued the company for breach of contract, with most of these cases being assigned to the federal court in Richmond, Virginia.

7. Westinghouse, by way of defence in these suits, pleaded commercial impracticability and also that it was the victim of a cartel, a 'club'. At about this time, documents taken from an Australian producer, Mary Kathleen Uranium, disclosed the producer meetings which had been conducted and their subject matter.

8. In defending the utility suits, Westinghouse tried to obtain evidence in England by letters of request directed to officers of Rio Tinto Zinc Limited, a British corporation affiliated with a number of the Canadian and Australian producers. In a case which went to the House of Lords, the British Courts refused to enforce the letters of request requiring the evidence.

9. At this point the scene shifts from one of commercial suits to one of antitrust suits. The Antitrust Division of the Department of Justice was under domestic pressure to take action against the alleged cartel, but it was also encouraged by some of the foreign governments concerned not to take action – on the grounds that the U.S. Government's protectionist actions had brought about the cartel, that uranium is a highly sensitive product comprehensively under government control and that, moreover, the cartel did not have a significant effect on the U.S. market.

10. The Antitrust Division, after much deliberation, brought a very limited action; a misdemeanor complaint against one U.S. company, Gulf Oil, and brought no action against foreign producers. Gulf paid a modest fine, thereby ending the Antitrust Division's involvement.

11. The battle royal is in the private lawsuit which was filed in Chicago in 1976 by Westinghouse against the foreign and U.S. producers under the Sherman Act and which seeks \$2 billion in damages trebled, plus attorneys' fees. Tennessee Valley Authority (TVA) brought a similar suit.

12. The foreign producers – some Canadian, some Australian, a South African company and the British company, RTZ, did not enter appearances to defend themselves against Westinghouse's suit and, in January 1979, Judge Prentice Marshall entered default judg-

ments against all of the foreign defendants. In Re: *Uranium Antitrust Litigation*, 473 F. Supp. 382 (N.D.Ill. 1979).

13. In a proceeding before Judge Marshall and again on appeal to the United States Court of Appeals for the Seventh Circuit, *amicus curiae* briefs were filed by the Governments of Canada, Australia, South Africa and the United Kingdom, urging that, on grounds of international comity, the defaults should not have been entered in this situation. The Court of Appeals refused to set aside the defaults, but did rule that the damages against the defaulting defendants should not be assessed until the case against the appearing defendants had been heard. In Re: *Uranium Antitrust Litigation* 617 f. 2d 1248 (7th Cir. 1980).

14. In the meantime a number of those appearing defendants had been failing to comply fully with Westinghouse's discovery requests. The defendants' justification was that they were complying with the foreign laws forbidding the production of the documents located in those countries. Westinghouse moved for sanctions against these defendants under Rule 37 of the Federal Rules of Civil Procedure. As to some defendants, regarding whom bad faith was alleged, Westinghouse asked for a default judgment. As to other defendants, it asked that adverse findings of fact be made and that defences be stricken, The defendants, for their part, argued that they had to comply with the foreign 'blocking' statutes, that the court should not exercise jurisdiction here, and that, as defences, there were foreign acts of state and foreign government compulsion which had caused the alleged conduct. There also was another round of *amicus* briefs on these various issues.

15. Judge Marshall has spent several months hearing evidence and arguments as to sanctions, jurisdiction and other issues. He has indicated that he will rule on these issues sometime in the fall of 1980 – this will probably be followed by another round of appeals. But the judge has also vowed that he will bring the case to trial in September of 1981.

9.



# The anti-trust division strikes a bargain

## BUSINESS AND THE COURTS

BY A. H. HERMANN, Legal Correspondent

IN THE course of the past year, a number of countries adopted legislation protecting their companies against excessive inquisitiveness on the part of American anti-trust agencies and courts. They include Australia, Britain, France and New Zealand.

This protective legislation has put formidable obstacles in the way of American authorities when prosecuting important and influential foreign companies. A draft of a consent judgment* filed by the Department of Justice just before Christmas (and received in London this week) indicates, however, that the bright boys of the anti-trust division have found a way out, or at least have seen the light at the end of the tunnel. In short they propose to make a bargain with the foreign company, which would assure them for the next 10 years of continued influence on its behaviour and of continued access to its documents and records.

The proposed settlement should bring to an end a civil anti-trust suit filed by the Department of Justice a year ago against Societe Nationale des Poudres et Explosifs (SNPE) and Fayette Chemical Corporation of Wood Ridge, New Jersey. In a parallel anti-trust suit filed only a few days earlier, the Department is prosecuting Hercules Inc. In both cases the product is industrial nitro-cellulose which Hercules is alleged to have attempted to monopolise in the U.S., and for the sale of which SNPE is accused of having formed a cartel with other non-U.S. producers.

Industrial nitro-cellulose is used in combination with other chemicals as a bonding agent in various coatings. It forms attractive, smooth finishes after only a short drying time and has a wide use, ranging from wood, paints, textile, paper and printing to cosmetics (where it is used for fingernail polishes). Before July 1977 all the material used in the U.S. was produced by two companies—Hercules and E. I. du Pont de Nemours and Company, Inc.

In July 1977, Dupont announced that it would discontinue the production and sale of industrial nitro-cellulose at the end of 1977, so that Hercules was left as the only domestic producer of this material in the U.S. The production capacity of Hercules could not satisfy the entire domestic demand, and the exit of Dupont from the market opened up major opportunities to foreign producers, among whom SNPE was prominent.

According to the Department of Justice, the foreign producers did not want to spoil the market by competition and formed a "pool" for meeting the unsatisfied demand for nitro-cellulose in the U.S. In addition to SNPE, there were Spanish, Italian and German companies in the ring: Explosivos Rio Tinto, Societa Italiana Prodotti Espodenti (SIPE), Mazzuchelli Celluloide S.P.A., Bofors, and Wassag Chemie GmbH. These companies appointed Fayette as the pool's agent.

Not all the members of the original pool took part in its operation. Bofors withdrew at an early date and other pool members did not sell in the U.S. But SNPE and SIPE did, and their prices were stabilised at the same level as the prices of Hercules and of the German company, Wolff Walsrode A.G.

The Department of Justice alleges that SNPE and Fayette conspired with others to fix and maintain prices at a non-competitive level, that they have in this way restrained competition in the U.S., and deprived U.S. purchasers of industrial nitro-cellulose of the possibility of competing for supplies in an open market.

This complaint could lead to very long litigation in the U.S. courts, during which many secrets of the companies concerned would be disclosed, while at some stage or other the Department of Justice would antogonise even further the authorities of the home countries of the foreign suppliers.

The proposed final judgment agreed between the parties has, therefore, many advantages for both: it saves long litigation, avoids disclosure, and does not provide any factual or legal basis for private suits under which, according to U.S. law, the parties harmed by the cartel could ask for treble damages.

The great charm of a consent judgment of this type is that it does not constitute any evidence against the accused party nor any admission by that party with respect to any issue of fact or law. But the judgment may not be entered until the court finds that it is in the public interest. The proposed judgment may be further modified as a result of comments submitted to the Department of Justice within a 60-day period.

Such comments, together with the Department's responses, will be filed with the court and published in the federal register. The Deparment of Justice remains free to withdraw its consent prior to entry of the judgment, and both parties may apply to the court later for any order necessary for the modification, interpretation, or enforcement of the judgment.

The proposed final judgment prohibits SNPE from agreeing with other parties, directly or indirectly, any restriction of supplies of industrial nitro-cellulose for the U.S., allocation of customers, fixing of prices or terms of sale, and the use of a joint sales agent or distributor. It also prohibits SNPE from providing, or obtaining from, other producers information concerning prices and sales, unless such information has been previously made available to the trade at large.

Fayette will be prohibited from acting as an agent or sub-agent for more than one producer of nitro-cellulose, but it will be allowed to buy the product on its own account from any producer as long as there is no agreement or understanding concerning Fayette's resale prices.

The judgment goes to great length to ensure that all officers and employees of the defendants are acquainted with the obligations imposed by the judgment. All such persons or agents of the company responsible for the sale of the product in the U.S. have to be furnished with a copy of the final judgment and with a statement specifying the criminal and civil penalties which may be imposed on such persons for its violation.

The statement has to warn the employees of disciplinary action to be determined by the company concerned and make it clear that the company's legal advisers are available for consultation. Whenever an employee or agent is replaced, the successor has to be furnished with the same information within 30 days. Moreover, copies of the final judgment have to be supplied by the defendants to a number of nitro-cellulose producers.

Finally—and this is how the Department of Justice hopes to overcome the barriers erected by the protective legislation mentioned at the beginning—SNPE undertakes (subject to any legal privilege) to supply the Department on written request, with account books, correspondence and other documents, and to submit written reports (under oat if requested) relating to its compliance with the obligations imposed by the judgment. It will be obliged to provide access to its premises and to allow U.S. officials to interview its employees.

SNPE will also be obliged to give notice before engaging in any transactions prohibited by the judgment but required by the laws of the country where such transactions have to take place. Should it be impossible to give such advance notice, the Department of Justice would need to be informed as soon as possible afterwards, and at least within 30 days.

The only concession SNPE seems to have won is that the obligations and information requirements stipulated in the judgment will not apply to nitro-cellulose intended for military use.

* *U.S. District Court for New Jersey Civil Action No. 80-149 before Judge Herbert J. Stern. Stipulation filed December 19, 1980, unreported.*

# 10. Procedural problems with regard to the Extraterritorial Application of EEC Antitrust Law

BERLIN 1980 MARIO SIRAGUSA

**Point 1. A Short Summary of EEC Antitrust Proceedings**

The procedure for the application of Articles 85 and 86 of the Treaty of Rome by the Commission of the European Communities (the 'Commission') is laid down in Council Regulation 17/62 and in the two Commission Regulations 27/62 and 99/63.

The Commission can start a procedure basically in three ways:

(i) Upon an application for a negative clearance (Regulation 17/62, Article 2) or an exemption (Regulation 17/62, Article 4);

(ii) following a third party complaint (Regulation 17/62, Article 3 (2)); or

(iii) on its own initiative, through individual procedure *ex officio* (Regulation 17/62, Article 3) or a general inquiry into a sector of the economy (Regulation 17/62, Article 12).

*A. Requests for Information*

The Commission has the power to obtain all necessary information from the governments and competent authorities of the Member States and from the enterprises (Regulation 17/62, Article 11 (1)). When sending a request for information to an enterprise, the Commission is required to forward a copy of the request to the competent authorities of the Member State in whose territory the seat of the enterprise is located (Regulation 17/62, Article 11 (2)).

*Informal request*: (Regulation 17/62, Article 11 (3)). The parties are not obliged to respond to an informal request. If they do respond and supply incorrect information, they are subject to fines ranging from 100 to 5,000 U.A. (Regulation 17/62, Article 15 (1) (b)).

*Formal request*: (Regulation 17/62, Article 11 (5)). If the parties do not respond to an informal request within the time limit fixed by the Commission, or if they supply incorrect information, the Commission has the power to require the information by a formal decision. The decision requiring information is binding on the parties. Not only the furnishing of incorrect or misleading information, but also the non-compliance with the decision within the time limit fixed will subject the parties to a fine ranging from 100 to 5,000 U.A. (Regulation 17/62, Article 15 (1) (b)). In addition, the Commission may impose periodic penalty payments ranging from 50 to 1,000 U.A. per day (Regulation 17/62, Article 16 (1) (c)) to compel the parties to supply complete and correct information requested by formal decision.

When carrying out a general inquiry into a particular sector of the economy, the Commission may also request the enterprises to communicate to it all agreements, decisions or concerted practices that are exempt from notification by virtue of Article 4 (2) and Article 5 (2) of Regulation 17 (Regulation 17/62, Article 12 (2)).

*B. Power of Investigation*

The Commission may undertake all necessary investigations of enterprises. To this end, the officials authorized by the Commission are empowered (Regulation 17/62, Article 14 (1)):

a. to examine the books and other business records;
b. to take copies of or extracts from the books and business records;
c. to ask for explanations on the spot;
d. to enter any premises, land and means of transport of the enterprise.

Officials of the competent authority of the Member State in whose territory the investigation is to be made may, at the request of such authority or of the Commission, assist the officials of the Commission in carrying out their duties (Regulation 17/62, Article 14 (5) ).

*Investigation under Article 14 (2) of Regulation 17/62.* The parties are not obliged to submit to an investigation carried out under Article 14 (2) of Regulation 17/62. However, if they do and produce the required books or other business records in incomplete form, they are subject to fines ranging from 100 to 5,000 U.A. (Regulation 17/62, Article 15 (1) (c) ). The Commission shall inform the competent authority of the Member State in whose territory the investigation is to be made of the investigation and identity of the authorized Commission officials in sufficient time before the investigation.

*Investigation under Article 14 (3) of Regulation 17/62.* Under Article 14 (3) of Regulation 17/62, the Commission has the power to order an investigation whether or not it has first attempted to submit the parties to an investigation carried out under Article 14 (2) of Regulation 17/62. The parties are obliged to submit to an investigation ordered by decision of the Commission. If they refuse to submit to the investigation or produce the required books or other business records in incomplete form, they are subject to fines ranging from 100 to 5,000 U.A. (Regulation 17/62, Article 15 (1) (c) ). In addition, to compel the parties to submit to the investigation the Commission may impose periodic penalty payments ranging from 50 to 1,000 U.A. per day (Regulation 17/62, Article 16 (1) (d) ). The Commission shall order the investigation after consultation with the competent authority of the Member State in whose territory the investigation is to be made (Regulation 17/62, Article 14 (4) ). Where an enterprise opposes an investigation ordered by the Commission, the Member State concerned shall afford the necessary assistance to the officials authorized by the Commission to enable them to make the investigation (Regulation 17/62, Article 14 (6) ).

*Investigation under Article 13 of Regulation 17/62.* At the request of the Commission, the competent authorities of the Member States shall undertake the investigations which the Commission considers necessary under Article 14 (1) or which it has ordered by decision pursuant to Article 14 (3). The officials of the competent authorities of the Member States responsible for conducting the investigation shall exercise their powers upon production of an authorization in writing issued by the competent authority of the Member States in whose territory the investigation is to be made. If so requested by the Commission or by the competent authority of the Member State in whose territory the investigation is to be made, the officials of the Commission may assist the officials of such authority in carrying out their duties.

### *C. Imposition of Fines*

The Commission may by decision impose fines ranging from 1,000 to 1,000,000 U.A., or a sum in excess thereof but not exceeding 10% of the turnover in the preceding year of each of the undertakings participating in the infringement, where, either intentionally or negligently (Regulation 17/62, Article 15 (2) ):

a. they infringe Article 85 or Article 86; or

b. they commit a breach of any obligation imposed by a decision granting an exemption under Article 85 (3).

The Commission may by decision impose periodic penalty payments ranging from 50 to 1,000 U.A. in order to compel the enterprises (Regulation 17/62, Article 16 (1) ):

a. to put an end to an infringement of Article 85 or Article 86;

b. to refrain from any act prohibited under Article 8 (3) of Regulation 17 (breach of obligations attached to an exemption under Article 85 (3) or abuse of the exemption).

The Commission may also impose fines ranging from 100 to 5,000 U.A. if the enterprises supply incorrect or misleading information in an application for a negative clearance or an exemption (Regulation 17/62, Article 15 (1) (a) ). It may also impose fines and periodic payments in order to enforce its power to request information and carry out investigations as described above.

The decisions taken pursuant to Article 15 (1) and (2) are not of a criminal law nature (Regulation 17/62, Article 15 (4)).

**Point 2. The Commission has the right to send informal requests for information to enterprises located outside the territory of the Community. The Commission probably also has the right to send a formal request for information to an enterprise situated outside the Community**

Pursuant to Article 11 (1) of Regulation 17/62, the Commission may obtain all necessary information from enterprises or associations of enterprises. The powers granted to the Commission are thus not expressly limited to enterprises located within the Community. The requirement under Article 11 (2) of Regulation 17/62, to the effect that before sending a request for information the Commission shall at the same time forward a copy of the request to the competent authority of the Member State in whose territory the seat of the enterprise is located, should not be read to imply a general limitation, or a limitation to the effect that a request for information to an enterprise outside the Community may be sent only to enterprises that belong to a group whose legal seat or principal place of business is within the Community. The requirement is simply a specific application of the general principle established in Article 10 (2) of Regulation 17/62, according to which the Commission shall carry out any procedure for the application of Articles 85 and 86 in close and constant liaison with the competent authorities of the Member States and such authorities shall have the right to express their views upon such a procedure.

Indeed, the Court seems to have implicitly recognized the Commission's power to send a request for information to enterprises located outside the Community. In its decision in *United Brands (Chiquita)* (Case 27/67, [1978] ECR 207), the Court, reviewing the Commission's finding on excessive prices, stated that '[t]he Commission was at least under a duty to require UBC to produce particulars of all the constituent elements of its production costs' (paragraph 256, at 302). While the facts of the case do not clearly emerge from the text of the Court's decision, the Court seems to refer to information which was held by UBC outside the Community, since it would have included production costs in Central America and transfer prices. (See pp. 244-245). It may be noted, however, that since UBC's subsidiary within the Community was also involved in the proceedings, it is arguable that the Court only referred to the Commission's power to request a company within the Community to supply the Commission with information located outside the Community (see Point 4. below).

Since no EEC measure would limit the Commission's powers in this regard, it would seem that any limitation on the Commission's right to send a request for information to enterprises outside the Community would have to be found in rules of international law rather than in the EEC rules.

The Commission's power to send an informal request for information to enterprises outside the Community should not create a problem under international law. The enterprises are not obliged to respond, and the Commission's request therefore could not be considered an attempted act of coercion.

Nevertheless, it should be noted, as mentioned in Point 1.A. above, that even an informal request for information pursuant to Article 11 (3) of Regulation 17, has two precise legal effects which might raise questions under international law. First, if the enterprises outside the Community respond, but supply incorrect information, they are subject to fines. Second, a request for information by a formal decision of the Commission, pursuant to Article 11 (5) of Regulation 17, must be preceded by the sending of an informal request for information. Thus the informal request for information is a necessary step in the formal procedure and thus it could be considered a part of it. It appears that the Commission has developed a practice of sending completely informal requests for information, *i.e.*, those which do not contain any reference to Article 11 (3) of Regulation 17, and which, therefore, would not seem to have the effects mentioned above.

In fact, it is normal practice for the Commission to send an informal request for information to enterprises outside the Community, without going through the authorities of the countries where the enterprises are located and seemingly without informing the authorities of its request. Generally, companies located outside the Community do answer the

Commission's informal request for information, although there probably have been cases in which no answer was submitted. It seems, for example, that in the *Zoja/Commercial Solvents* case (O.J. No L 299/51, December 3, 1972), CSS did not answer an informal request for information.

It is more difficult to determine whether international law would limit the power of the Commission to send a formal request for information to enterprises outside the Community. Although a formal request for information would, according to Regulation 17/62, empower the Commission to impose fines or periodic penalty payments in the case of non-compliance or upon finding that the information is incomplete or misleading, the sending of the formal request for information would not seem in itself to constitute an act of coercion which is exercised outside the territory of the Community in such a way as to be incompatible with international law. Indeed, to the extent that the Commission has substantive jurisdiction on the basis of the effects doctrine (a jurisdictional basis not yet explicitly recognized by the Court), it would seem reasonable that the Commission should have the right to send formal requests for information to enterprises outside the Community. However, in light of the possible imposition of fines in the case of non-compliance, and quite apart from the question of service of process (see Point 5. below), it would seen appropriate for the Commission to inform the authorities, and in particular the office of foreign affairs, of the country where the enterprise is located.

In practice, the Commission seems not to have sent a formal request for information to an enterprise outside the Community.

International law would seem to limit the Commission's power to request information from any enterprise outside the Community if furnishing the information would amount to a violation of the law of the country where the enterprise is located. The Commission does not seem to accept this point of view, as witnessed by the decision in the *CSV* case, which is commented upon in Point 4. below.

Finally, non-compliance by an enterprise located outside the Community with a Commission's informal or formal request for information might affect the position of the enterprise in the proceedings before the Commission or, more likely, in the proceedings before the Court. With respect to the proceedings before the Commission, should the enterprise choose to furnish the information requested, it would probably be free to do so before the end of the proceedings, for instance, after having received the statement of objections or at the oral hearings. Should the enterprise seek review before the Court of a decision taken by the Commission, it is likely that non-compliance with the Commission's request of information might place a heavier burden of proof on the enterprise. The Commission's decision would be based on facts obtained from sources other than the enterprise concerned and, although there seem to be no cases in point, it is likely that the Court would impose strict standards of proof on the enterprise. It would seem inappropriate for the Court to refuse to consider facts presented by the applicant on the grounds that these facts had not been revealed in response to the Commission's request of information. It is interesting to note that, in the field of breach of the Commission of due process, the Court held in *Hoffmann-La Roche (Vitamins)* (Case 85/76 [1979] ECR 461) that procedural irregularities committed by the Commission could be remedied in the course of the appeal. *A fortiori*, it seems reasonable to conclude that the applicant should be free to choose at which level of the procedure to disclose facts relevant to its defense.

**Point 3. The Commission has the power to impose fines on enterprises located outside the Community who submit incomplete information, in an answer to an informal request for information or who do not comply with a formal request for information or who submit incorrect or misleading information. The Commission may also impose periodic penalty payments in order to compel an enterprise located outside the Community to supply complete and correct information requested by formal decisions. The enforcement of the decisions imposing these fines or periodic penalties can be made only against assets which are located within the Community**

The Commission's powers with respect to the imposition of fines or periodic penalty payments in relation to informal or formal requests for information, summarized under Point 1. above, are applicable to enterprises located outside the Community in the same way as to those located within the Community. However, the enforcement of the decisions imposing fines or periodic penalty payments on companies outside the Community can be made only against assets located within the Community and belonging to that enterprise.

The Commission has never issued a decision imposing fines or periodic penalty payments in relation to a request for information to an enterprise located outside the Community.

**Point 4. The Commission has the power to obtain all necessary information, without any limitation as to the place where the information is located**

Pursuant to Article 11 of Regulation 17/62, the Commission may obtain all necessary information from enterprises or associations of enterprises. Regulation 17/62 does not limit the Commission's power to obtain information to that which is located within the Community. The absence of specific provisions for the supply to the Commission of data located abroad should imply that the Commission has the power to obtain all necessary information, without limitation as to the place where the information is located. Three different situations can be distinguished, however:

(i) It seems clear that the Commission has the power to require information which is located outside the Community, but which is under the control of an enterprise located within the Community, for instance, if the information is with a subsidiary outside the Community of a group whose headquarters are within the Community.

(ii) If the information is outside the Community, but the group which controls the information is present within the Community, *e.g.*, through a subsidiary, the Commission should also have the power to obtain the information. On the basis of the economic unit theory, the group is held to be present within the Community and therefore the situation should not be different from that under (i) above. As mentioned in Point 2. above, the Court, in *United Brands (Chiquita)*, seems to imply that the Commission has the power to require information located outside the Community which is under the control of a non-EEC group, at least when the group has a subsidiary within the Community. Whether the request for information should be addressed to the subsidiary within the Community or to the parent company outside the Community does not seem to be important. In any event, if the Commission issues a formal request for information which is not complied with, the enforcement of fines or periodic penalties would be made against the assets of the subsidiary within the Community.

(iii) When the information is under the control of a group which does not have an establishment within the Community, the issue is whether the Commission has the power to send requests of information, a question which has been treated under Point 2. above.

The Commission has to a certain extent dealt with these matters in the *CSV* case (O.J. No L 192/27, July 16, 1976), involving the 'Centraal Stikstof Verkoopkantoor', the Dutch joint selling agency for simple nitrate fertilizers. CSV was a party to an agreement bringing all European manufacturers of nitrate fertilizers together in Nitrex A.G., a company located in Zurich, Switzerland. CSV had refused to supply the information the Commission had requested because it considered that if this information included documents relating to the activities of Nitrex, those members of their staff who were also on the Nitrex Board of Directors could be regarded by the Swiss authorities as committing an offense under the Swiss penal code. Only in the event that the Commission issued a decision which was confirmed by the Court of Justice could such disclosure take place, because the staff members involved could then plead compulsion as a defense to any prosecution in Switzerland. The Commission issued a formal request for information, finding the reason given by CSV for refusing to comply with the request unacceptable. The Commission pointed out that the information requested concerned the business activity of the Dutch firm belonging to CSV and of CSV itself, that such information was available within the Community, and that the Commission was entitled to request it. The fact that the information had been furnished to a body governed by Swiss law did not mean that it could no longer be supplied to the Commission. The Commission added that 'even if Swiss law could be interpreted to mean that the supply of information to the Commission amounted to unlawful disclosure, this would still not warrant delay in the performance of obligations imposed by the Commission in order to enforce the rules of competition'.

**Point 5. A decision is properly served under EEC law when it reaches the addressee and puts the latter in a position to take cognizance of it. No special form is required for service of process outside the Community**

The second paragraph of Article 191 of the Treaty of Rome provides that 'decisions shall be notified to those to whom they are addressed and shall take effect upon such notification'. The Court considers that, to the extent that the addressee of the decision has been put in a position to take cognizance of it, the decision is duly notified.

In a case involving the Treaty of Paris (Case 8/56, *Accierie Laminatoi Magliano Alpi (ALMA) contre Haute Autorité de la Communauté Européenne du Charbon et de l'Acier*, [1957] Rec. 179, 190), the Court held that where notification is required during the course of administrative proceedings, it is sufficient that the document of which notification is made should duly reach the inner structure of the addressee ('régulièrement entreé dans la sphère interne du destinataire').

In the *Dyestuffs* case (Cases 48/69, 52/69 and 53/69, *ICI, Geigy, Sandoz*, [1972] ECR 619, 787, 845, at 651-652, 825 and 849), the Commission had notified its decision to the subsidiaries located within the Community. The applicants argued that their subsidiaries had not been given any authority by the parent companies to accept the notification and that, under the applicable national law, the subsidiaries were under no duty to bring the documents in question to the attention of the parent companies. The Court held that irregularities in the procedure for notification of a decision do not invalidate the decision, but may in certain circumstances prevent the period within which an application to the Court must be lodged from starting to run. Pursuant to that third paragraph of Article 173 of the Treaty, the period for instituting proceedings for the annulment of individual measures of the Commission starts to run from the data of notification of the decision to the applicant or, in the absence thereof, from the data in which it comes to the knowledge of the latter. The Court thus stated that since it was established that the applicant had had full knowledge of the text of the decision and had exercised its right to institute proceedings within the prescribed period, the question of possible irregularities concerning the notification ceased to be relevant.

In *Continental Can* (Case 6/72 *Europemballage and Continental Can v. Commission* [1973] ECR 215, at 241 (paragraphs 9-10)), the applicant had argued that the decision should have been notified through diplomatic channels, while the applicant had only received one or two letters from the Commission by mail. The Court stated that '[A] decision is properly notified within the meaning of the Treaty, if it reaches the addressee and puts the latter in a position to take cognizance of it. This was so in the present case, because the contested decision actually reached Continental and the latter cannot make use of its own refusal to take cognizance of the decision in order to render this communication ineffective'.

Pursuant to Article 2(1) of Regulation 99/63, the Commission shall inform enterprises or associations of enterprises *in writing* of the objections raised against them. The communication shall be addressed to each of them or to a joint agent appointed by them. Pursuant to Article 2(2), the Commission may inform the parties by giving notice in the Official Journal of the European Communities if this appears appropriate, given the circumstances of the case, in particular where notice is to be given to a number of undertakings but no joint agent has been appointed. A fine or a periodic penalty payment may be imposed on an enterprise or association of enterprises only if the objections were notified in the manner provided for in paragraph 1, *i.e.*, in writing (Article 2(3)). There is no special provision for service of the statement of objections to an enterprise outside the Community.

With respect to the statement of objections, the Court followed the same approach it took with respect to decisions, considering that a statement of objections served in accordance with the EEC rules to a party located in a third country cannot invalidate the subsequent administrative procedure, once it is established that by enabling the addressee to take cognizance of the objections held against him it has achieved its purpose.

The Court took this approach in the *Dyestuffs* cases (Cases 52/69 and 53/69 (*Geigy, Sandoz*) [1972] ECR at 823-824 and 849). There the applicants complained that the Commission served the notice of objection in a manner inconsistent with Swiss law, the place where the notice was to be served, because the Swiss Confederation does not recognize the validity of service by post of a foreign measure of this kind on its territory. The applicants thus argued that the notice was null and void and that this irregularity gave rise to an infringement of the applicant's right to be heard. The Court held that the purpose of the notice of objections provided for in Article 2(1) of Regulation 99/63, is to enable those concerned to put forward their arguments in the context of proceedings initiated against them. The Court continued:

> 'Since there is no convention on the matter between the Community and the Swiss Confederation, the question of how this notice is to be served on interested parties established outside the territory of the Community depends on international practice and must be resolved with mutual regard to the spheres of jurisdiction both of the Community and of the third State concerned.
>
> It appears from the file that the authorities of the third State in question do not for the present envisage any practical possibility of service, considered by them to be valid under internal law, on the territory of that State.
>
> Therefore international law cannot be invoked in order to deny the Community the power to take the necessary steps to ensure the effectiveness of measures taken with a view to curtailing conduct adversely affecting competition which has arisen in the Common Market, even if the registered office of the undertaking responsible for such conduct is situated in a third country.
>
> Furthermore, the main purpose of the notice in question is to ensure that those concerned may exercise the rights which they enjoy under the Treaty and Community legislation.
>
> Therefore a notice served in accordance with Community rules cannot be considered to invalidate the subsequent administrative procedure if it must be served in a third country, once it is established that by enabling the addressee to take cognizance of the objections held against him it has achieved its purpose.'

One may speculate about what would happen in a case in which companies located in a country which had no convention with the Community on the service of process would have returned unanswered the letter received containing the Commission's objections. There would seem to be three options for the Commission. First, since by hypothesis the latter had reached the enterprise, the Commission could consider on the basis of the Court rulings in *ALMA*, in the *Dyestuffs* and *Continental Can* that 'by enabling the addressee to take cognizance of the objections held against him it has achieved its purpose', and that the addressee's refusal to take cognizance of the objections does not affect the validity of the notification. Second, if one of the EEC Member States did have a convention with the third country in question providing for specific procedures for the service of process, the Commission could require the authorities of the Member State to make the notification of the Commission's objections in the form provided for in the convention, on the basis of the general principle of cooperation between the Commission and the authorities of the Member States implicit in Regulation 17/62 (see in particular Article 14(b)). Finally, the Commission could publish the statement of objections in the Official Journal of the European Communities, pursuant to Article 2(2) of Regulation 99/63. In this case, pursuant to Article 2(3) of Regulation 99/63, the enterprise notified of the Commission's objections through the publication in the Official Journal would not seem to be subject to the imposition of fines.

**Point 6. The requirements of service of process would be met under EEC law if process is served on a foreign person or company through its controlled subsidiary or branch located within the Community. The requirements of service of process are also likely to be met if service of process is served through an independent agent within the Community, provided that the agent is under an obligation to inform the foreign entity**

As mentioned in Point 5. above, the Court in *ALMA* ruled that when the document to be notified reaches the internal structure of the addressee (*'la sphère interne du destinataire'*) the notification is sufficient. The applicant argued that the letter, due to some spelling errors in the address, had never reached the General Manager at the plant of the applicant. The Court held that, since it was proved that the letter had reached the legal seat of the enterprise (and had been delivered to an employee of the applicant) it was not relevant whether or not it had been transmitted to the plant of the applicant.

On the basis of this general rule it seems that the requirement of service of process would be met under EEC law if process is served on a foreign company though a controlled subsidiary. In fact, in the *Dyestuffs* case, with respect to the companies located outside the Community (Ciba, Geigy, Sandoz and ICI) the Commission notified its decision to their subsidiaries located within the Community, stating that since those subsidiaries were wholly controlled by their parent companies they were within the '*sphère interne*' of their parent companies (O.J. No L 195/11, August 7, 1969, at 16). As mentioned in Point 5. above, the Court rejected the applicant's contention that the notification was irregular, and held that since it was established that the applicant had full knowledge of the text of the decision and it had exercised its right to institute proceedings within the prescribed period, the question of possible irregularities concerning the notification ceased to be relevant. The Court thus did not find it necessary to rule whether notification to the wholly controlled subsidiaries within the Community constituted a regular notification and in particular as to whether notification to the controlled subsidiary meant a notification reaching the '*sphère interne*' of the parent company within the meaning of its ruling in *ALMA*.

Probably because of this uncertainty, but more likely because of the possible problems under international law, the Commission, in *United Brands (Chiquita)*, in deciding to notify its decision to UBC's controlled subsidiary within the Community, did not refer to the fact that the subsidiary was wholly controlled, but only to the fact that UBC had appointed its subsidiary as its representative in the proceedings (O.J. No L 95/1, April 9, 1976, at 19). The issue of notification was not raised in the proceedings before the Court.

Notification through a branch within the Community should raise no problem. A branch is formally a part of the foreign company, and depends for its continued existence on the company's existence. The constitution of a branch in a country makes the entire company subject, under ordinary rules of civil procedure, to service of process in that country, and therefore notification to the branch of a foreign company should clearly be held equivalent to notification of a company located within the Community. It is interesting to note that in Form A/B (the form provided by the Commission for the application for negative clearances and notifications), the Commission requires in its question I.6, if the enterprises are established or have their seat outside the territory of the Community, to state the name and address of a representative or *branch* established within the Community.

The notification to an independent agent within the Community should not in general be considered to meet the requirement of service of process. As mentioned above, Article 191 requires that 'decisions shall be notified to those to whom they are addressed and shall take effect upon such notification'. An independent agent could not normally be considered to be within the '*sphère interne*' of the foreign company, even though there is a tendency in EEC substantive laws to consider independent agents, in certain conditions, to be within the 'economic unit'. It would seem that only if the independent agent had a specific obligation to inform the foreign company of such notification, either because he had been specifically appointed as the representative of the foreign company in its dealing with the EEC authorities or because the agent was the general legal representative of the foreign company within the Community, would it be possible to consider that a service had been duly made on the party to whom the decision was addressed. As mentioned above, question I.6 in Form A/B requires the enterprise to state the name and address of *a representative* within the Community.

**Point 7. The application and enforcement of the EEC antitrust law does not seem to require personal jurisdiction over the person or company against which an antitrust proceeding is directed**

As mentioned in the Introduction, this report does not discuss the requirement of substantive jurisdiction for the extra-territorial application of EEC antitrust law. The case law indicates that the Commission's efforts to apply the EEC antitrust law extra-territorially rest basically on the principle of personality and on the principle of effect. Without entering into a discussion of which of these two principles should apply, it is sufficient to say that the question of personal jurisdiction becomes relevant only if the principle of effect is deemed to be sufficient to assert substantive jurisdiction for the extra-territorial application of the EEC antitrust law. In fact, should the principle of personality be deemed to be the one required to assert substantive jurisdiction, the requirement of personal jurisdiction would be redundant. The EEC law would then be applicable only to persons or companies having their seat within the Community over which, by definition, the Commission has personal jurisdiction.

On the assumption that substantive jurisdiction may be asserted on the basis of the principle of effect, it is important to determine whether personal jurisdiction is required in addition. Nothing in the applicable regulations would seem to require any criteria other than that of the substantive jurisdiction determined on the basis of the texts of Articles 85 and 86. For example, with respect to the application of Article 85, it is necessary that the three following conditions be met:

(i) the existence of an agreement or a concerted practice between enterprises or a decision of an association of enterprises;

(ii) an effect on trade between Member States; and

(iii) an effect on competition within the Common Market.

To the extent that the principle of effect is a sufficient basis for substantive jurisdiction, once the three conditions have been met, Article 85(1) would be applicable to companies located outside the EEC.

Perhaps because of the uncertainty as to whether substantive jurisdiction should be based on the principle of personality or on the principle of effect, the Commission sometimes seems to have relied on some elements of personal jurisdiction. For instance, in some cases the Commission has apparently taken the position that enterprises located outside the EEC submit themselves to the jurisdiction of the Commission by filing the agreement with the Commission, or even only by consenting that their participation in the agreement be mentioned in the application for a negative clearance or an exemption. The Commission seems to take the position that, by inviting the Commission to consider whether the agreement could be granted a negative clearance or an exemption under Article 85(3), those enterprises submit themselves to the jurisdiction of the Commission.

It can generally be said that the Commission's approach is by no means consistent at the present time. The matter thus requires further thought, in particular with respect to the possible effects of the filing of documents with the Commission in connection with a notification.

It is clear that the Commission's jurisdiction will depend on whether or not the requirements for substantive jurisdiction are met. Assuming that the Commission may assert substantive jurisdiction on the basis of the principle of effect, the Commission would have jurisdiction over an agreement between enterprises located outside the Community as long as the agreement has an appreciable effect on competition within the Community and on trade between Member States, whether or not the agreement has been notified. If the principle of effect is appropriate for substantive jurisdiction, it would seem absurd to limit the Commission's substantive jurisdiction to those agreements which have been notified. It therefore seems clear that participation in a notification to the Commission is not relevant to the question of whether the Commission has jurisdiction with respect to a certain agreement or practice.

On the other hand, it would be interesting to inquire whether participation by a non-EEC enterprise in a notification could affect the Commission's power to enforce the EEC antitrust law *vis-à-vis* that enterprise – in other words, whether, because of the notification, the Commission would be in a position to take actions which it otherwise could not have taken. This would seem to directly involve the question of personal jurisdiction. The answer appears to be the same as in the case of substantive jurisdiction: the notification would seem to have no effect. To the extent that the Commission's power of enforcement is limited under international law, because it would constitute an act of coercion to be exercised on the territory of a sovereign state, the fact that the non-EEC enterprise participated in the notification cannot affect the limitations imposed by international law. It is the sovereign state itself which, for instance through the conclusion of a convention, can consent to the exercise of an act of coercion by a foreign institution on its territory, and not an individual, even if its participation to the notification could be construed as a consent on its part to submit itself also to the Commission's coercive acts of enforcement. It therefore seems clear that, in the absence of an international convention, the Commission cannot exercise its power of investigation under Article 14(2) of Regulation 17 in a non-EEC country (see Point 8. below), without regard to whether the enterprise subject to the investigation has participated in a notification or has otherwise consented to the Commission's scrutiny of its activity.

Similarly, the Commission could not sue in the courts of a non-EEC country in order to recover amounts due for fines or periodic penalty payments, whether or not the enterprise took part in a notification (see Point 3. above). With respect to formal requests for information, as mentioned in Point 2. above, international law does not seem to limit the Commission's power to send such requests to enterprises outside the Community. The fact that the request is sent in relation to an agreement in the notification of which the non-EEC enterprise has participated would therefore not seem to be relevant. In such cases, the Commission, when informing the authorities of the country where the enterprise is located of its formal request for information, could appropriately mention that the inquiry relates to a notified agreement and that the non-EEC enterprise participated in the notification.

**Point 8. Although the Commission has been given the power to undertake all necessary investigations, investigations outside the Community would seem to be in violation of international law. However, to the extent that a Member State has the power to conduct an investigation in a non-EEC country, the Commission may request the authorities of that Member State to conduct an investigation in that country**

Pursuant to Article 14(1) of Regulation 17/62, the Commission may undertake all necessary investigations in carrying out the duties assigned to it by Article 89 and by provisions adopted under Article 87 of the Treaty. The powers granted to the Commission are thus not expressly limited to investigations carried out within the Community. The provisions of Article 14(2) of Regulation 17/62 on informal investigations, requiring the Commission to inform the competent authority of the Member State in whose territory the investigation is to be made, and of Article 14(4) of Regulation 17/62 on formal investigations, requiring the Commission to consult with the competent authority of the Member State, should not be considered to limit the power of investigations to those carried out within the Community. Those provisions, like those contained in Article 14(5) and (6) of Regulation 17/62, regulate only the investigations conducted within the Community and are specific applications of the general principle established in Article 10(2) of Regulation 17/62 of close and constant liaison between the Commission and the competent authorities of the Member States.

However, the exercise of the Commission's power of investigation outside the Community would seem to constitute a violation of international law, unless exercised in the framework of a treaty or of an agreement between the Community and the country where the investigation is conducted. An investigation of the premises of an enterprise located outside the Community would necessarily appear to constitute an act of coercion exercised in the territory of a sovereign state in violation of international law. It would not be relevant whether the enterprise located outside the Community whose premises were to be investigated belonged to a group whose headquarters were within the Community. While the Commission could obtain the information located abroad through a request addressed to the companies of the group established within the Community (see Point 4. above), conducting the investigation abroad would constitute a violation of the sovereignty of the country in which the office investigated was located.

As mentioned in Point 12. below, the Community is not party to any treaty or agreement with non-EEC countries which would allow the Commission to conduct investigations in countries outside the Community to apply EEC antitrust rules. Thus, until any such treaty or agreement is concluded, the Commission cannot conduct any investigation for the purposes of the application of EEC antitrust law outside the Community. In fact, it seems not to have attempted to do so.

Another possibility exists, however. Pursuant to Article 13(1) of Regulation 17/62, the Commission has the power to request the competent authorities of the Member States to undertake the investigations which the Commission considers to be necessary under Article 14(1), or which it has ordered by decision pursuant to Article 14(3). Unfortunately, no guidelines have yet been established as to the way in which the Commission may exercise its powers under Article 13(1). Although this provision refers mainly to investigations to be carried out by the competent authorities in the Member States in whose territory the investigation is to be made, the powers granted to the Commission are not limited in this respect. Thus, to the extent that a Member State has been given certain powers of investigation in a non-EEC country, pursuant to a treaty or other agreement which it has concluded with that country, it is not excluded that the Commission would request the competent authorities of that Member State to exercise those powers in connection with an investigation which the Commission considers to be necessary under Article 14(1) of Regulation 17.

In such a case, it would, of course, be necessary to ascertain whether all the conditions for the exercise of the Member State's power of investigation had been met. In particular, it would be necessary to determine whether the power of investigation of the Member State could be exercised in a proceeding relating to the application of the EEC antitrust rules. Since the EEC antitrust rules are part of the internal legal system of all the EEC Member States and may be directly applied by the competent authorities and the courts of all the Member States, it may be likely that the powers of investigation of the Member State could be considered broad enough to cover an investigation directed to the application of the EEC rules. Nevertheless, one should consider that the investigation may express the foreign company to the fines or periodic penalty payments provided by Regulation 17/62, which may be imposed exclusively by the Commission. One should thus also consider whether the exposure to such risk is acceptable under the treaty or other agreement which gives the Member State the powers of investigation.

In this context, it may be relevant whether the alleged violation of the EEC antitrust rules under investigation has an effect on competition within the Member State which the Commission has requested to carry out the investigation. First, when the practice under investigation affects competition within the Member State which has been requested to carry out the investigation, the legitimacy of such an investigation under the relevant treaty or other agreement is less likely to be contested. Second, the practice under investigation may also constitute a violation of internal antitrust rules of the Member State and thus be subject to the imposition of fines by the competent authorities of that Member State. In such a case, the practice under investigation would already have exposed the non-EEC company to the imposition of fines. Although the investigation may result also in the imposition of fines by the Commission, the additional risk of fines is somewhat limited by what the Court stated in *Wilhelm v. Bundeskartellamt* (Case 14/68, [1969] ECR 1 at 15):

> 'If, however, the possibility of two procedures being conducted separately were to lead to the imposition of consecutive sanctions, a general requirement of national justice, such as that expressed at the end of the second paragraph of Article 90 of the ECSC Treaty, demands that any previous punitive decision must be taken into account in determining any sanction which is to be imposed.'

The reports on national law will consider in their answer to Point 12. what are, if any, the multilateral or bilateral agreements for mutual cooperation in transnational antitrust investigations to which the Member State may be party.

**Point 9. EEC law does not provide for the right of the defendant or witness to be heard outside the Community**

Article 19 of Regulation 17/62 and Regulation 99/63 laying down implementing provisions concerning hearings does not specify where such hearings will take place. The organization of the hearings is left to the discretion of the Commission on the basis of the provisions of Regulation 99/63. Article 8(1) provides that the Commission shall summon the persons to be heard to attend on such date as it shall appoint. Furthermore, pursuant to Article 8(2), Member States may appoint an official to take part in the hearings. The hearings shall be conducted by the persons appointed by the Commission for that purpose (Article 9(1)). So far all the hearings have been conducted by Commission officials.

On the basis of these provisions and the fact that the hearings are an intrinsic part of the administrative procedure, the possibility of holding hearings outside the Community seems to be excluded.

**Point 10. Enterprises located outside the Community have performed acts outside the Community as a result of decisions taken by the Commission or the Court. No enforcement of any such decision has been attempted outside the territory of the Community**

Enterprises located outside the territory of the Community have performed acts outside the Community which were ordered by the Commission or resulted from a Commission decision. For instance, the imposition of a fine on a company located outside the Community results in an order to perform an act, the payment of the fine, outside the territory of the Community. The Commission has imposed fines on companies located outside the Community, but no enforcement of any such decision has been attempted outside the territory of the Community.

**Point 11. The few cases of extra-territorial application of EEC law seem to show an uncooperative attitude on the part of the national authorities or civil servants of the foreign country**

No decided case involving extra-territorial application of the EEC law mentions that assistance was given to the Commission by the authorities or civil servants of the foreign country. On the contrary, there are indications that, in general, the attitude of these authorities or civil servants has been uncooperative.

In the *Dyestuffs* cases (Cases 48/69, 52/69 and 53/69, *ICI, Geigy, Sandoz*, [1972], at 635, 792, 803 and 804), there are several references to the hostile attitude of the British and Swiss authorities. The Commission revealed that both the British Ambassador (at 635) and the Swiss Ambassador (at 803) refused to forward notification of the decision to a subsidiary established within the Common Market. With respect to the communication of the statement of objections, the Federal Department of Political Affairs in Bern took the position that public international law permits a sovereign state to refuse acceptance of notification by post (at 792). The Federal Department of the Swiss Police recommended to the Commission an alternative course: it should invite the foreign company to elect domicile on EEC territory with a view to a possible notification and, should the company refrain from doing so, bring to its attention the consequences which would follow from this refusal (at 804).

**Point 12. Mutual cooperation between the Commission and some non-EEC countries could take place in the framework of the OECD. Although some informal cooperation takes place, in particular between the US and the Canadian authorities and the Commission, the Commission has been unwilling to aid the enforcement of US antitrust rules against European companies. If the anti-competitive behavior has an effect on trade between the Community and certain EFTA and other countries, consultation between the Commission and the authorities of the country in question may take place under the relevant treaty**

On October 5, 1979, the Council of the Organization for Economic Cooperation and Development (OECD) issued a Recommendation on cooperation between member countries on restrictive commercial practices affecting international trade. This recommendation supersedes the two previous recommendations issued by the Council on October 5, 1967, and on July 3, 1973 (*Ninth Report on Competition Policy of the European Communities*, point 33).

The 1979 Recommendation provides for the notification, exchange of information and coordination of the enforcement proceedings of the OECD Member countries with respect to restrictive commercial practices affecting international trade. The Recommendation also provides for consultation between those member countries affected by the restrictive commercial practice and those which may be concerned by enforcement proceedings brought by other member countries. If a satisfactory solution has not been found, the interested Member States may submit the case to the Experts Committee on Commercial Restrictive Practices for conciliation.

The Commission participates in the OECD's work at a multilateral level and also has regular bilateral contacts with national authorities in the United States and Canada, and occasionally with authorities in other countries. In the *Eighth Report on Competition Policy*, (point 43, see also page 14), the Commission stated:

> 'Developing its cooperation with the competition authorities of non-member countries, which it considers essential if similar points of view on the measures to be taken to combat restrictive practices affecting international trade are to be arrived at, the Commission continued to exchange non-confidential information on competition issues of mutual interest with the American antitrust authorities. Similar arrangements have now been agreed to with the equivalent authorities in Canada.'

Although the relations between the Commission and the U.S. antitrust authorities have been relatively close for a number of years, the U.S. authorities' attempts to expand this cooperation do not seem likely to succeed at the moment. In a letter sent by Dr. Schlieder, Director General of the Directorate General on Competition (IV) of the Commission, in February 1978, to Mr. Shenefield, his counterpart in the U.S. Department of Justice, the Commission indicated rather clearly that the U.S. objective of increased contacts and cooperation between the two agencies is subject to limitations. It is reported that the letter contained the following text:

> 'The Commission's direct powers vis-à-vis enterprises in the Common Market are confined to the application of Community law. The problems which would arise from the application of American antitrust legislation to those enterprises concern the sovereignty of Member States.'

Nothing in Dr. Schlieder's letter suggests that the Commission is opposed to cooperation in respect of restrictive practices infringing both the EEC Treaty and U.S. antitrust rules, but it appears unlikely that the Commission would be willing or able to aid the enforcement of U.S. antitrust rules against European companies.

The position taken by Dr. Schlieder in his letter to Mr. Shenefield may have influenced the reply given by the Commission to a parliamentary question by Mr. Cousté, who asked whether the Commission would make contact with the U.S. antitrust authorities with a view to easing the participation of U.S. subsidiaries in crisis cartels. The Commission stated that it saw

> 'no need for a special arrangement with the American antitrust authorities to allow European subsidiaries of American companies to take part in consultations which are a standard practice in dealing with Community problems. If however, for fear of proceedings under American antitrust legislation, these firms prefer not to take part in such consultations, the Commission can only abide by this decision.' (Answer to Written Question 109/78, OJ No C 157/19, July 3, 1978.)

The Commission may have thought that approaching the U.S. Antitrust Division on the lines suggested by the questioner would have appeared to be inconsistent with the Commission's earlier position that, in effect, each authority should concern itself with enforcing its own law, and should not look for the help of the other when it comes to extraterritorial enforcement. One may also speculate, of course, that the Commission did not see how consultation with the U.S. authorities could help, since no U.S. exemption or special regulation could be expected.

One of the EEC Member States has entered into a cooperation agreement with the United States: U.S. antitrust authorities (the Antitrust Division of the U.S. Department of Justice and the Federal Trade Commission) and German antitrust authorities (the Federal

Minister of Economics and Federal Cartel Office) entered into an Agreement of Mutual Cooperation regarding Restrictive Business Practices on June 23, 1976.

The agreement provides that the antitrust authorities of the two countries will cooperate and render assistance to each other in connection with:

a. antitrust investigations or proceedings;

b. studies related to competition policy and possible changes in antitrust laws; and

c. activities related to the restrictive business practices work of international organizations of which both parties are members.

As mentioned in Point 8. above, bilateral or multilateral cooperation agreements to which EEC Member States are parties might offer the Commission a basis for requesting the competent authorities of the Member States to undertake an investigation which the Commission might consider necessary for the enforcement of EEC law.

The free trade agreements between the Community and the EFTA countries (Austria, Finland, Iceland, Norway, Portugal, Sweden and Switzerland) and the agreement with Israel contain provisions which are similar to the rules of competition of the EEC Treaty. To the extent that any restrictive practice affects trade between the Community and the signatory country, each of the two contracting parties may bring the matter to the attention of the Joint Committee set up under the agreement and thereafter adopt safeguard measures. The Joint Committee should be presented with all the relevant information with a view to seeking a solution acceptable to the contracting parties.

**Point 13. To the extent that the restrictive practice has an effect on competition within the Community and on trade between Member States, the Commission seems to have the power to order the resident of the Community involved in such a practice to do or to refrain from doing acts outside the Community. No such order has ever been issued**

Pursuant to Article 3(1) of Regulation 17, where the Commission finds that there is an infringement of Article 85 or Article 86, 'it may by decision require the undertakings or association of undertakings concerned to bring such infringement to an end'. This provision has been broadly interpreted by the Court in *Commercial Solvents v. Commission* (Cases 6 and 7/73 [1974] ECR, 223 at 255), in which the Court stated:

> 'This provision must be applied in relation to the infringement which has been established and may include an order to do certain acts or provide certain advantages which have been wrongfully withheld as well as prohibiting the continuation of certain action, practices or situations which are contrary to the Treaty.'

Although it is not yet clear whether the same broad injunctive power that the Court recognized in connection with an Article 86 violation would apply with respect to violations of Article 85, it seems clear that this injunctive power is not limited to orders to do or to refrain from doing acts within the Community. To the extent that an infringement of EEC law has been held to exist, and thus an effect on competition within the Common Market and on trade between Member States has been found, the Commission seems to have the power to order a resident of the Community (or, for this matter, a non-resident) to do or to refrain from doing acts outside the Community. Except for in the circumstances mentioned in Point 10. above, no such order has ever been issued.

Such an injunctive power seems to be indirectly confirmed by the Court in a recent decision (Case 22/79, *Greenwich Films/Sacem*, October 1979; OJ No C 292/10, November 21, 1979), in which the Court approved the potential application of Article 86 to contracts between nationals or residents of one Member State which are implemented outside the Community. The question put to the Court was whether SACEM, the French organization which has the contractual right to deal with authors' rights relating to musical works, was abusing its dominant position in violation of Article 86 by imposing on its members the assignment of their worldwide rights.

The Court dealt exclusively with the question of whether trade between Member States could be affected by the implementation in third countries of contracts entered into in one Member State by its national or its residents. The Court referred to its judgment in *Commercial Solvents v. Commission*, in which it established the principle that, in order to determine whether trade between Member States was affected by an abuse of a dominant position, the effect of the abuse on the competitive structure of the market within the EEC has to be taken into account. In this respect, there is no distinction between products to be sold within the EEC and products to be exported to third countries. The Court added that this principle applies not only to trade in goods but also to the supply of services, such as the management of copyrights.

In a very brief opinion, which unfortunately does not coherently explain the Court's thinking, the Court found that organizations managing musical copyrights and exacting royalties may conduct their activities in such a way as to result in a partitioning of the Common Market and in obstacles to the freedom of services. Their activities may have these consequences even if the management of copyrights relates, in certain cases, to the performance of musical works in a third country, and therefore Article 86 can be held applicable.

The case raises the important question of whether the Court of Justice is setting a new and more sweeping basis for the jurisdiction of Community law, by giving a broader interpretation to 'effects on trade between Member States' that it has until now. In any event, the case seems at the very least to show a willingness on the part of the Court to consider the effects on the competitive structure within the EEC even when the alleged abuse in the case at issue involves only a restriction on activities outside the EEC. Thus, to the extent that the activities outside the EEC are deemed to have an effect on trade between Member States, an order to bring them to an end would seem to be within the powers of the Commission.

**Point 14. EEC law does not provide for protection of Community nationals or residents against actions of foreign antitrust authorities**

While some Member States have taken steps to protect their nationals or residents against actions of foreign antitrust authorities, no such protection is afforded under EEC law. As mentioned under Point 12. above, Dr. Schlieder in his letter to Mr. Shenefield stated that '[t]he problems which would arise from the application of American antitrust legislation [to] enterprises [in the Common Market] concern the sovereignty of Member States'.

**Point 15. Reactions of foreign governments in cases involving extraterritorial application of EEC law have been mentioned under Point 11. above**

See Point 11. above.